YOUR PSYCHOLOGY DISSERTATION

Sara Miller McCune founded SAGE Publishing in 1965 to support the dissemination of usable knowledge and educate a global community. SAGE publishes more than 1000 journals and over 800 new books each year, spanning a wide range of subject areas. Our growing selection of library products includes archives, data, case studies and video. SAGE remains majority owned by our founder and after her lifetime will become owned by a charitable trust that secures the company's continued independence.

Los Angeles | London | New Delhi | Singapore | Washington DC | Melbourne

YOUR PSYCHOLOGY DISSERTATION

Emily Harrison and
Panagiotis Rentzelas

Los Angeles | London | New Delhi
Singapore | Washington DC | Melbourne

Los Angeles | London | New Delhi
Singapore | Washington DC | Melbourne

SAGE Publications Ltd
1 Oliver's Yard
55 City Road
London EC1Y 1SP

SAGE Publications Inc.
2455 Teller Road
Thousand Oaks, California 91320

SAGE Publications India Pvt Ltd
B 1/I 1 Mohan Cooperative Industrial Area
Mathura Road
New Delhi 110 044

SAGE Publications Asia-Pacific Pte Ltd
3 Church Street
#10-04 Samsung Hub
Singapore 049483

Editor: Donna Goddard
Editorial assistant: Marc Barnard
Production editor: Victoria Nicholas
Copyeditor: William Baginsky
Proofreader: Sharon Cawood
Indexer: David Rudeforth
Marketing manager: Camille Richmond
Cover design: Wendy Scott
Typeset by: C&M Digitals (P) Ltd, Chennai, India

© Emily Harrison and Panagiotis Rentzelas 2021

First published 2021

Library of Congress Control Number: 2020934871

British Library Cataloguing in Publication data

A catalogue record for this book is available from the British Library

ISBN 978-1-5264-9729-1
ISBN 978-1-5264-9728-4 (pbk)

Contents

Index of Tables

Index of Figures

About the Authors

 **Dr Emily Harrison** is a Senior Lecturer in Psychology at Birmingham City University. Her main research interests are concerned with understanding how children acquire and develop literacy skills, namely reading, phonological awareness and speech rhythm sensitivity. Emily studied for her undergraduate degree and her PhD at Coventry University, where she conducted her dissertation in the area of reading development, investigating the relationship between reading skills and speech rhythm sensitivity. Her PhD later investigated the effectiveness of a rhythmic-based reading intervention for enhancing literacy skills in children. Emily has worked at Birmingham City University since September 2015, where she is currently the Deputy Course Director on the BSc (Hons) Psychology programme and leads multiple modules, including the undergraduate dissertation module.

As dissertation coordinator, I hope to inspire developing researchers. I always look forward to guiding students through the module and helping them to conduct a project that they can be proud of. The dissertation is something you should enjoy, so manage your time well, set yourself a time-plan and stick to it, and don't underestimate how long each process will take. Each and every one of you has the potential to succeed.

 **Dr Panagiotis (Panos) Rentzelas** is an Associate Professor in Social Psychology and Director of Internationalisation for the School of Social Sciences at Birmingham City University. Prior to his appointment, Panagiotis was employed as a Post-Doctoral Research Fellow in Social Psychology at the University of Essex and as a Policy Advisor/Scientific Officer for an international organisation. Panagiotis holds a PhD in Psychology from the University of Nottingham and a BSc (Hons) in Psychology from the University of Essex. Panagiotis' research lies in the area of experimental social psychology, cross-cultural and contextual cognitive differences and human motivation.

I am really excited about the textbook that you are holding in your hands. It has been created keeping your needs in mind and is designed exclusively for final-year psychology students studying for their dissertation. One of the reasons that we wrote this book is because we want to help you enjoy this module as much as we did when we were undergraduate students. This is your best chance to put into practice everything that you have learned throughout your undergraduate studies and to create a dissertation project that belongs to you. I hope that you will enjoy this textbook and find it useful throughout the module.

Acknowledgments

We would like to express our gratitude and thanks to our students and colleagues, past and present, for their support on the dissertation module at Birmingham City University, and in particular during the production of this textbook. We hope that this textbook will be useful to both students and staff.

We would like to thank colleagues at Sage for their ongoing support, encouragement and constructive feedback.

Finally, a special thanks to you, as the reader, for taking the time to read our advice and guidance throughout this book.

Online Resources

Your Psychology Dissertation comes with some excellent student resources to help you plan and write your dissertation. You can access them at: **https://study.sagepub.com/harrisonandrentzelas**

These student resources include:

- A **dissertation planner** to manage your time, featuring a customisable checklist to manage the progress of your dissertation.
- Printable **meeting logs** to take useful notes of supervisor feedback.
- A useful **reference table** to keep track of your sources as you go along.
- Easy-to-use **participant information**, consent and **debriefing sheet** templates to make your study preparation so much quicker.
- A **responding to formative feedback** sheet to help you make the most of the advice you receive.
- Mock **presentation questions** to help you prepare for any presentations you might do as part of your course.

GETTING STARTED

Welcome to your psychology dissertation!

In this part of the book, we will introduce you to your dissertation module, provide you with an overview of how to use this book, and discuss how to get started by exploring the literature and devising an appropriate research question for your study.

1

Welcome to Your Dissertation!

Learning outcomes

By the end of this chapter you will:

- Understand what a dissertation is all about
- Become familiar with the way this textbook works and how it can help you during your project
- Be prepared for the journey this book will take you on and be able to identify the links between your prior learning and your dissertation project
- Be able to identify the transferable, employability-related skills you develop while working on your dissertation and how to apply them to the job market.

1.1 What is a dissertation?

The dissertation is an independent research project and is ultimately the most important assessment you will complete whilst at university. Typically, it will be completed in the final year of your undergraduate studies, but dissertations are also an important part of many master's courses, too. The dissertation builds upon prior learning from your Research Methods module(s) earlier in your course, and takes the form of a large lab report, which can be quantitative and/ or qualitative in nature. The dissertation will utilise skills and knowledge learnt in multiple areas of your psychology course.

In completing your dissertation, you will need to design, conduct and write up an ethical and well-constructed (i.e. well designed, justified, conducted and reported) research project that meets the learning outcomes of your course. You will need to be able to demonstrate an ability to work independently, to manage the relationship with your supervisor, and to critically evaluate your own work. You may be required to complete a research proposal, which takes the form of a project plan, in which you will need to justify the decisions you make during the planning process. By pre-registering your research question, hypothesis and proposed methodology, you will prepare yourself for the data collection, analysis and writing-up processes. Before you can collect any data for your project though, you will also need to gain ethical approval from your university ethics committee; it is important that you consider ethics *throughout* the planning process. Ethical approval is a legal and moral obligation of all research, and we will explore this more in Chapter 9.

Top tip!

> Start thinking about ethics now. It is important that you consider ethics throughout the planning process, when making decisions about study design. Ethics are not just there to mitigate risks that arise as a result of decisions that were made earlier!

The final dissertation will comprise a comprehensive literature review, rationale for your project, research question(s) and/or hypotheses, methodology (including an overview of your design, participants, materials and procedure), data analysis and results, and a discussion chapter, supported with references and relevant appendices. The overall word count of your dissertation will vary depending on your course specification but will usually be between 6,000 and 10,000 words. One of the biggest and most useful pieces of advice for managing your dissertation is to break it down into manageable chunks – work backwards from your deadline to identify dates by which you want to have achieved certain milestones, such as submitting your ethics application, collecting data and completing draft chapters. Your department may set out formative deadlines for you throughout the module, or they may have some flexibility in allowing you to set these in collaboration with your supervisor. Either way, get these dates in your diary from the start of the module, so that you have a structure to work to. This will allow you to work on one thing at a time to avoid the stress of multitasking and managing competing deadlines.

Top tip!

> Break your work down into manageable chunks – work on one thing at a time and plan your time effectively so that you can focus your attention and energy efficiently.

1.2 The difference between essays/coursework and your dissertation

The obvious difference between your dissertation and any other piece of coursework you have completed in the past is the length of it – your dissertation will be considerably longer than your standard 2,000-word essay or lab report that you might have completed for other modules on your course. But the dissertation also differs in other ways – you will be required to demonstrate a deeper level of understanding of your chosen topic area than would perhaps have been required in the past. Designing and conducting your own research project requires a sophisticated level of understanding and expertise in terms of existing literature, research methodology and data analysis. You will need to demonstrate that you have thought about how your ideas 'fit in' with existing literature in your chosen topic area and what your contribution to knowledge is. Whilst you might have worked on a set project for your coursework in the past, the dissertation gives you much more flexibility to manage your own project: you will need to demonstrate originality and creativity, whilst also considering the practical applications of your findings. Finally, greater emphasis will be placed on the importance of establishing 'flow' in your writing, generating a clear story throughout your dissertation.

1.3 Enhancing your employability

The dissertation module is pivotal in utilising and further developing many academic and transferable skills, such as understanding research papers, critically discussing literature, academic writing, constructing an argument, research design, data collection, data analysis, building professional working relationships, working independently, adhering to ethical standards, time management and working to deadlines, all of which are important skills in a psychology graduate. Throughout this textbook, you will see that we have highlighted the employability-related skills that will be enhanced through the tasks involved in the development of your dissertation – this will help you to understand how to apply the skills you have developed on your course (and particularly on the dissertation module) to the job market.

Key transferable skills developed through your dissertation

Communication skills – written and verbal

The dissertation module helps to develop your communication skills in a number of ways. Firstly, your dissertation assessment requires you to write clearly and concisely, communicating

(Continued)

5

your ideas and findings clearly to the reader within your written dissertation. Secondly, during the process of conducting your dissertation, you will need to communicate with your supervisor, stakeholders and participants. You will need to be able to communicate effectively in writing (e.g. via email and in your ethics documents), and verbally (in supervisory meetings and, if doing a face-to-face study, during data collection). Your verbal communication skills are further developed through dissemination of your findings to fellow students and staff – this may be informally, or as part of a more formal verbal presentation.

Critical thinking

Your dissertation module requires you to think critically about your own work and the work of others. In your literature review, you will need to critically discuss existing research, leading to the identification of your own research question(s) and design. You will also need to critically evaluate your own methodology and findings in the discussion chapter of your dissertation.

Problem solving

By identifying a research question in your literature review chapter, you are identifying a 'problem' or 'gap' within our current understanding. By designing your research to provide an answer to your research question, you are creating a solution to the problem, addressing the issue in mind and extending current knowledge.

Decision making and reasoning

Designing and conducting research requires you to make many decisions. Within your dissertation, you will not only need to explain these decisions, but you will also need to *justify* the decisions that were made during the design and implementation of your project. Being able to develop a strong rationale for your project relies on your ability to justify and reason clearly.

Building professional working relationships

During your dissertation, you will need to build a professional working relationship with your supervisor, with your participants and with any key stakeholders in your project (e.g. gatekeepers or wider organisations involved in the research). Being able to build, manage and maintain these relationships is an important employability skill that will be vital for the workplace.

Working independently

As well as being able to build professional working relationships with others, employers will also be looking for you to demonstrate your ability to work well independently, to self-motivate and to plan, to organise and to manage your time effectively. Your dissertation is pivotal in developing these skills: as an independent project, your dissertation requires you to work independently of other students, and to manage your own time and workload – organisation is key to success! Completing your dissertation alongside your other modules and commitments also demonstrates an ability to manage your time effectively to meet competing deadlines.

1.4 How to use this book

The dissertation project can often seem quite daunting – it is totally normal to feel a bit overwhelmed by the prospect of producing such a large piece of work. But help is here – *Your Psychology Dissertation* is designed to guide you through the process of designing, conducting and writing up your independent psychology research project, from before the module begins through to your submission date and beyond.

Completing your dissertation can also make you feel quite isolated as every project is different – even if you and your friend are doing your dissertations in the same area of psychology, the chances are that you will have completely different research questions and methodologies. But whilst dissertation students have a tendency to feel isolated in their research, you won't be alone in this journey. You will most likely be allocated a supervisor from the department with whom you will work closely on your project. They will provide you with one-to-one support, advice and guidance throughout the dissertation process, so it's important to know how to manage your relationship with them. Chapter 2: Managing the Relationship with Your Supervisor provides guidance on how to build a professional working relationship with your supervisor and what to expect from them.

Chapter 3: Choosing a Research Topic provides guidance on identifying a suitable topic for your dissertation, and Chapter 4: Understanding the Literature provides guidance on how to conduct effective literature searches, read effectively and narrow your focus. Once you have settled on a topic and read around the area, Chapter 5: Developing Your Rationale, Research Question(s) and Hypothesis; and Choosing between Quantitative and Qualitative Research Design will help you to start designing your project. Once you have identified the area you want to investigate, your next task is to think about what questions you want to answer. Your choice of question(s) and how you word them will usually map on well to a specific type of research design (quantitative or qualitative), so Chapter 5 will help you to consolidate your ideas to identify a viable direction for your project. It's also really important that you are able to justify the decisions you make throughout the process of designing and conducting your dissertation, so this chapter will help you to develop your rationale.

Once you have decided on a general direction for your project, Chapter 6: Quantitative Methodology and Chapter 7: Qualitative Methodology both focus on designing your project in more detail – these chapters focus on identifying data collection techniques, and the practicalities of working with participants. Most undergraduate dissertations will be either quantitative or qualitative, but a small number of students may decide to design and conduct a mixed methods study. Chapter 8: Mixed Methods Research Projects details the practicalities of designing and conducting both types of research within a single study.

Once you have decided on the research question(s) and methodology for your study, you'll then begin thinking about collecting data – but before you can do this, you will need to gain ethical approval from your department or faculty research ethics committee. It is important that you think about ethics *through-out* the process of designing your study, as you will need to ensure that the decisions you make regarding your design are ethical. Your module leader or your supervisor will be able to provide you with more information about the process of gaining ethical approval at your institution, but the general principles are the same for all researchers. Chapter 9: Ethical Considerations will discuss generic and specific ethical principles outlined by the British Psychological Society and will explain how to go about designing and conducting your project in an ethical manner.

Once you have collected your data, the next step is to prepare your data and run your data analysis. Chapter 10: Quantitative Data Analysis and Chapter 11: Qualitative Data Analysis will guide you through the basics of preparing for and conducting your data analysis for both qualitative and quantitative projects. You can combine the information from both of these chapters to help with mixed methods projects. It would be impossible for us to cover all data analysis techniques in these chapters, so we advise that you combine this information with your core research methods textbooks.

Throughout the dissertation module, most departments offer the opportunity to submit drafts of certain chapters of the dissertation for formative feedback from your supervisor. Throughout this process, you will need to pay careful attention to your writing style. Chapter 12: Writing Style focuses on writing academically, providing some tips to help you consolidate your existing writing skills and apply them to your dissertation. In the final dissertation, you will need to demonstrate 'flow' between the existing literature, your rationale, your research question(s), your design, data analysis *and* the discussion of findings, so it is advisable to think about this throughout the module, not just at the writing up stage.

The discussion chapter is where this all comes together and can often be perceived as being a difficult chapter to write. Nevertheless, this is your time to shine, so try to think of it as an opportunity to show us what you can do, rather than a challenge. Chapter 13: Writing the Discussion Chapter and Preparing for Submission will guide you through the process of producing a great discussion chapter. Chapter 13 will also help to make sure that you've included everything you need in the final dissertation and formatted your work correctly, ready for submission.

Finally, Chapter 14: Communicating Research: Preparing Manuscripts, Posters and Talks helps you to think about life after submitting your dissertation. If you're thinking about publishing your research, you will need to consider how to transform your dissertation into a journal article. You might also consider presenting your research at a conference – on campus at your own institution, through the BPS at a student conference or in the wider field at a national or international conference in your specialised area. If this is something you like the sound of, you'll need to consider how to extract information from your dissertation and transform it into a conference poster or oral presentation. This final chapter will provide you with guidance on dissemination of your research and help you to recognise the benefits of your dissertation to your own professional development.

Throughout the book, you will see that learning outcomes are provided at the start of each chapter, clearly highlighting key objectives throughout the process of completing your dissertation. Chapter summaries and easy-to-use checklists are included at the end of each chapter, providing an opportunity to track your progress, help you plan ahead and manage your time effectively. This book is aimed specifically at students on BPS (British Psychological Society) accredited BSc single and joint honours psychology programmes, and builds upon material and content covered at earlier stages in your course, whilst also focusing attention on new material specific to your dissertation.

Our philosophy in writing this book is not just to guide you through the dissertation process, but also to help you to develop and recognise the importance of the research-related skills and transferable employability-related skills that you have developed throughout your undergraduate degree and throughout the dissertation module. As such, you will also see that the book includes short exercises on research-related soft skills, and employability boxes highlighting employability-related skills that you are developing by completing certain activities. In some chapters, you will also see frequently asked questions, which will help to clarify points of uncertainty.

1.5 Where to begin

The first step in designing your dissertation project is deciding on a topic that you want to investigate. Most institutions are fairly flexible in allowing you to conduct your dissertation in almost any area of psychology (subject to ethical approval and access to participants), but you should certainly discuss your ideas with your supervisor first. Your supervisor is likely to be an experienced researcher and it is important that you make the most of the supervision opportunities available to you throughout the module. We will discuss how to manage the relationship with your supervisor in Chapter 2. If you haven't already met them, we advise booking an appointment as soon as possible.

Chapter 3 will then help you to start thinking about how to transform your interests into a topic for investigation. We will also discuss literature searching, identifying a gap and devising your research question in more detail.

1.6 Time management

The key to success in your dissertation is to plan, organise and manage your time effectively to complete key milestones on time – for example, gaining ethical approval, collecting your data and completing draft chapters. Common barriers to completing milestones include:

- Not understanding/appreciating the importance of careful planning
- Delays in gaining ethical approval
- Failure to allow sufficient time to write up relevant chapters
- Difficulties/delays with participant recruitment
- Lack of self-motivation

It is important that you recognise that whilst these are common issues in the research process, they are also barriers that can be avoided through careful planning and organisation. If you feel that you are the sort of person who leaves things to the last minute, try setting yourself manageable goals and timetabling study time specifically for the dissertation module. Breaking your work into manageable chunks will help to make it seem less daunting.

Chapter summary

The dissertation is an independent research project, taking the form of an empirical research report consisting of four main chapters: a comprehensive literature review, methodology, results and discussion. The dissertation must involve the collection of empirical research data that can be analysed and written up in the final report.

The dissertation module is pivotal in helping you to develop key employability skills, including communication skills, critical thinking, problem solving, decision making, reasoning, building professional working relationships and working independently.

The dissertation is the largest and most important assessment you are likely to complete whilst at university, and will need to be completed alongside your other modules and assessments. The key to success is being able to organise and manage your time effectively.

Checklist

✓ Familiarise yourself with the content of your dissertation module: Read your module guide, check out the online resources and familiarise yourself with the assessment strategies involved.

✓ Plan your time: Look over the key dates for your module. When are you expected to have completed draft chapters? When should you aim to submit your ethics application? When do you want to begin/complete collecting data?

✓ Produce a mind map of the areas of psychology that have interested you most on the course so far: Are there any topics that you are particularly passionate about?

✓ Book an appointment with your project supervisor to discuss your ideas so far and narrow your focus.

2

Managing the Relationship with Your Supervisor

Throughout the dissertation, you will be working closely with your supervisor on all aspects of your project. Your dissertation supervisor is there to advise you, provide guidance and expertise, but it is your job to manage your relationship with them. This chapter will provide guidance on working with your supervisor, how to make the most of your supervision and how to manage the student–supervisor relationship.

Learning outcomes

By the end of this chapter you will:

- Understand what it means to be 'independent' in your work
- Know what to expect from your supervisory relationship
- Understand the importance of building a professional working relationship with your supervisor
- Know how to make the most of your supervision
- Be able to prepare for supervisory meetings and keep effective notes.

2.1 The dissertation as an 'independent' research project

Throughout your dissertation module, and indeed in many sections of this book, you will be reminded that your dissertation is an 'independent' research project – your department might even use the word 'independent' within the dissertation module title. In order to succeed in this independent project, it is first important that you understand what is meant by the term 'independent'. You will be expected to design, conduct and write up your own independent project, but it is important to recognise that there is a big difference between working independently and working alone. Working completely independently (i.e. alone) indicates a lack of any supervision or input from others, but this is not the case with the dissertation. Whilst it is important to take ownership of your ideas, your design and your data, you will need to regularly communicate and work with your supervisor throughout the processes involved in completing your dissertation. You will need to demonstrate that you are able to work individually and that you can manage your own time effectively to meet your deadlines, but also that you can seek advice and guidance when they are required. Building rapport with your supervisor is incredibly important, as we will discuss later in this chapter, and you will be expected to keep in regular contact with them throughout the module.

Top tip!

Don't misinterpret 'independent' as meaning that you can't seek advice. Keeping in regular contact with your supervisor is imperative for your progress and success.

2.2 The supervisory relationship: What to expect

Your supervisor is there to provide advice and guidance at all stages of the dissertation process, as and when needed. This might include providing support in making key decisions, such as choosing a suitable topic, identifying a suitable research question and deciding on appropriate methodology. They will be able to help you refine your ideas, point you towards relevant literature or search terms, provide guidance on accessing and recruiting participants, and support you in running and interpreting your data analysis. However, as identified in section 2.1, it is important that you are able to demonstrate your ability to work independently and you will therefore be expected to have a go before seeking guidance, and come prepared to supervisory meetings. As we will discuss later in this book, it is important that you are able to justify your decisions throughout the designing and conducting of your dissertation, so if you seek guidance on making these decisions, it is important that you understand where this guidance is rooted, and that you are able to scientifically justify your rationale, your research question(s), your research design and your data analysis in your writing.

Your supervisor will not just be there to guide you when it comes to making decisions about your study though. They are also there to provide you with constructive feedback – allowing you the opportunity to improve your work and achieve the best possible mark you can. In return, your supervisor will expect you to use your initiative to plan and prepare for meetings, to ask questions where necessary, and to respond and follow up on feedback. This includes feedback received in meetings as well as written feedback, so it is important that you make notes in your meetings and keep a log of the things you have discussed (see sections 2.5.1 and 2.5.2 for details on preparing for meetings).

2.2.1 Constraints on supervision

Whilst it is important that you understand what to expect from the supervisory relationship, it is also important to recognise the limits that might be placed upon the amount and type of supervision you can receive. There are a myriad of different academic supervision models in practice across academia, ranging from collective and peer supervision to more traditional one-to-one supervision. The most common type of supervision is the conventional dyadic supervisor–student model (McCallin & Nayar, 2012), which we will focus on throughout the course of this chapter and later in the book. Whilst this one-to-one supervision is common practice across the higher education sector, it is likely that your department will have additional, more specific, regulations and practices. Some departments may put limits on how much time a supervisor can spend with a dissertation student, or even have learning agreements in place that provide a rigid framework of how supervision can function. It is important to recognise that even individual supervisors will have individual supervisory styles and prefer-ences for the type and frequency of contact that you have with them, and it is important to respect their differences as researchers rather than see this as a barrier to seeking and receiving support. We advise that you discuss the regula-tions, timeline and requirements of your dissertation module with your supervisor and agree together on an approach that works for both of you within the con-straints of the module. You should discuss this, together with the expectations that you and your supervisor have of one another, at your first meeting with your supervisor. We will discuss this further in section 2.4, but first we must consider the process by which a supervisor is allocated to you.

2.3 Supervisor allocation

Individual departments and institutions have different processes when it comes to allocating students to supervisors for their dissertation. Whilst some departments involve students in this process by allowing them to choose a supervisor, other departments allocate students on the basis of a research proposal or topic choice, whilst others might not provide any choice at all. In some departments, students are in control of the process of choosing a topic, whilst in other departments it is common practice for supervisors to govern this process. It is important that you understand and respect your department's position on this, so read on for an overview of both approaches.

2.3.1 Choosing a supervisor

If your department lets you choose your supervisor, you should invest time in preparing for this process. You should pay careful attention to your department's academic staff list (usually available on the department or faculty webpage) and the research interests of individual members of staff, in order to identify potential supervisors. If you can, locate some of their papers and read their research in more detail – this will help you not only to identify a potential supervisor, but also to narrow your focus when it comes to identifying a topic area or research question for your project. Most departments will also hold regular research seminars, which are usually open to students, and attending these will give you further insight into the research areas of your lecturers. If you have the opportunity, it is also worth talking to as many staff members as possible to determine how your research interests might align with theirs, and also to find out about their supervision style and any restrictions when it comes to the number of students they can supervise. This will help you to understand what to expect in terms of the likelihood of being allocated to them, and what to expect in the longer term regarding supervision practices.

It would be beneficial to choose a supervisor whose research interests align with yours, whether this relates to the topic area or the methodology or both. For example, if you want to do a dissertation project on critical social psychology using qualitative research techniques, approaching a member of staff who is a cognitive psychologist with expertise in mathematical modelling would not be advisable. If your ideas align with the expertise of your supervisor, it is more likely they will be able to provide you with targeted, useful, expert advice on all aspects of your research project.

Homework

Create a list of potential supervisors and read their research. Look for published papers that they might have authored and see how they match your dissertation ideas.

It is also important to recognise that the vast majority of academic staff will be more than capable of supervising undergraduate projects in all areas of psychology and using a range of research methods. You might also identify potential supervisors for your project by considering their reputation as a tutor. Consider which members of staff you get along with, or those you have found interesting and helpful in other modules of your course to date. Selecting a supervisor with whom you have already built some rapport will help you to build an effective working relationship later on.

2.3.2 Receiving an allocation

As we have already identified, individual departments and institutions have different processes when it comes to allocating students to supervisors for their dissertation. Many departments will not provide students with the opportunity to select a supervisor for their project, and this is often for good reason. This is particularly true for larger departments, where it is unlikely that students will be familiar with all members of staff who are available to supervise dissertation projects. If your department does not offer you a choice of supervisor, they might offer you a choice of topic instead. You may be asked to complete a topic choice form or to submit a research proposal on the basis of which you will be allocated to a suitable supervisor. This may or may not be the person you would have chosen if offered a choice, but it will allow your department to identify the most suitable supervisor for each student's project whilst also controlling the demand and workload of individual members of staff, ensuring that they have the capacity to provide you with adequate supervision. Remember, academic staff have a range of responsibilities, including their own research as well as leading modules and supervising students. Workload can put constraints on the number of students that each member of staff can supervise, and giving students a choice often results in the small number of staff that students have had previous contact with being overwhelmed by requests for supervision. Allocating students on the basis of an idea, rather than a preference for *who* they work with, can be an effective way to ensure fairness across the department's students and staff. In some cases, departments may not allow students to make *any* choices regarding their dissertation supervisor or topic. In these cases, it is common for supervisors to suggest or stipulate that their students conduct their research project in a particular area of psychology or using specific methodologies. If this is the case in your department, it is important not to be discouraged by this approach to allocation. This is often implemented in order to increase the compatibility between the project a student conducts and their supervisor's expertise. Nevertheless, it is important to remember that the dissertation is *your* research project, and you will need to take ownership of it, taking the project in a direction of your choosing within the constraints that your supervisor might set.

Frequently asked questions

What should I do if I don't know who I want to work with, or I don't know what topic I want to research at the allocation stage?

Start by trying to narrow down your ideas (Chapter 3 provides some suggestions on how to do this) to come up with a topic area you're interested in. Next, look into the research interests of members of staff in your department – see if something here interests you further. Finally, don't worry if you want to change your ideas later, as the vast majority of supervisors will be more than capable of supervising projects in all areas of psychology, at least at undergraduate level. Once you receive an allocation, your supervisor will be able to comment on your ideas and make suggestions for taking your ideas to the next step in designing your project.

What should I do if I get allocated to a supervisor whose interests don't align with my own?

How you approach this will depend on your department's policy towards supervision practices. Some departments might place emphasis on the student choosing the topic, whilst others might place emphasis on the supervisor suggesting a project to the student. If you have flexibility in choosing and designing your own project from scratch, you should be mindful of the fact that the vast majority of supervisors will be more than capable of supervising projects in all areas of psychology. If, on the other hand, you do not have such flexibility, you should speak to your supervisor as soon as possible to express your concerns and try to come to an agreement over your research topic and/or methodology. Your module leaders will also be able to provide further advice, depending on your individual circumstances.

2.4 The importance of building a professional working relationship with your supervisor

Once you have been allocated to a supervisor for your project, you will need to work on building a working relationship with them. This is important for a number of reasons. Firstly, you will be working with them throughout the module, which is likely to last the duration of your academic year. Building rapport with them early on will make this process easier and more enjoyable for both of you. Secondly, the relationship you build with your supervisor is likely to influence the way in which you communicate with one another. You need to be comfortable with your supervisor in order to feel at ease asking questions and in receiving constructive feedback. Sometimes, you might disagree with the feedback your supervisor provides, or you might even find yourself questioning *their* work. It is important not to be phased by these experiences, as these are all important for the development of your critical discussion skills – a key employability skill.

Frequently asked questions

What should I do if I disagree with the advice my supervisor has given me?

Talk to them about it: ask them to explain why they have given the advice they have. If you still disagree, seek a second opinion, without undermining the advice your supervisor has provided. Your supervisor will have good reasons for having given it, and remember that they will be marking your work, so don't contradict this advice without (a) fully understanding why it was provided, and (b) being able to justify your reasons for wanting to do things differently.

What if things aren't working in the relationship with my supervisor?

In some cases, as with any relationship, the supervisory relationship might sometimes not work out. Your module leaders will be able to provide further advice, depending on your individual circumstances, and it is important that you speak to them as early as possible if you have concerns about your supervision so that any issues can be resolved appropriately.

Further to the benefits of building a strong working relationship with your supervisor during the dissertation module, you should also consider the wider implications of the relationship on your future development as a researcher and your employability. For example, if you decide to try to publish your dissertation, the supervisory relationship will extend beyond the dissertation module in that your supervisor will become your collaborator. We will discuss the process of planning and preparing for publication in Chapter 14 of this book, but for now you should be aware that it can be a lengthy process. If you wish to do this, you will need to maintain the relationship with your supervisor not just during the dissertation module but also beyond graduation.

Finally, consider that your supervisor will have worked more closely with you on your dissertation than perhaps any other member of staff has worked with you on any other aspect of your course. They are likely to have had more contact hours with you than any of your other lecturers, and the nature of contact will have been very different. In your experience to date, it is likely that you will be used to a more traditional relationship, involving minimal contact with your lecturers during lectures, seminars and lab work. The interaction that you have had with members of staff in these contexts will have been structured within the context of a specific module. With the dissertation, things are a little different. The dissertation has an element of scholar apprenticeship, where you are working and studying under the auspices of an experienced academic. Consequently, the relationship that you develop with your supervisor is more of a continuous educational process that progresses throughout your project. As such, by the end of your project, your supervisor will have developed a clear idea of how you work, how you communicate, and the standard of work you produce. As a result, they are likely to be a person you might approach for a reference to support your applications for postgraduate study or your future career.

EMPLOYABILITY
TIP!

The nature of contact you have with your supervisor will be very different to the contact you have experienced with members of staff earlier in your studies. You will be working closely with them throughout your dissertation, and, as such, they will develop a clear idea of how you work, how you communicate, and the standard of work you produce. As a result, they will be best placed to provide a reference for you – so building a strong working relationship is vital.

2.5 How to make the most of supervision

By this point in the chapter, you should have an idea of what supervision is, understand what to expect from supervision, and understand the importance of building a professional working relationship with your supervisor. Next, it is important to understand how to *use* your supervision effectively in order for you and your work to benefit. In this section, we will discuss how to make the most of the supervision available to you. The first step is to consider how to prepare for your initial meeting with your supervisor.

2.5.1 Preparing for your initial meeting

Your first meeting with your supervisor is where you can start to develop the working relationship. In order for you both to know what to expect from this relationship, it is a good idea to use this first meeting to set out the expectations that your supervisor has of you, and that you have of them. You should discuss the supervision style you are expecting, when and how you envisage that you might need support, and when and how to expect feedback. As we mentioned earlier, your department might put a limit on the amount of supervision time you can receive as part of the module – if this is the case, you should discuss during your initial meeting how you plan to use this time effectively throughout the module. Your supervisor will have significant experience of supervising student projects, so they might have suggestions for the most effective way to use some, or all, of your supervision time. For example, you might want to plan meetings to discuss each of the key sections of the dissertation, such as the ethics application, your literature review, methodology and results. We suggest you discuss your needs and vision for supervision with your supervisor and plan your meetings ahead of time so that you have some dates in your diary. Similarly, you should consider how to organise your study time effectively throughout the module in order to meet certain milestones. Within the dissertation module, your department might have scheduled opportunities for you to submit sections of your work for formative feedback. In contrast, some departments will be more flexible, allowing students to set dates for formative submissions with their supervisor. This is something else that you should discuss at your first meeting, so that you and your supervisor can both get some dates in your diaries and know what you are working towards.

Your first meeting is also the place where you will need to bring your supervisor up to date on your project ideas. What topic(s) are you interested in researching? Your supervisor will want to know your topic interests, and importantly what motivated you to choose this topic (e.g. personal interest, interests in particular aspects of your course, your strengths). This is important in order to ensure that you and your supervisor can come to an agreement over your project. If you want to impress your supervisor at this stage, you will need to demonstrate that you are prepared for your dissertation and that you have already conducted some wider reading. As we have discussed earlier, your supervisor may or may not be an expert in your topic of choice, so they may want you to explain what we already know about this topic. The next thing you will need to discuss is what you actually want to *do* in your project. What question(s) might you aim to answer in your project? How might you go about doing this? Have you thought about what design you might want to employ? Are there any ethical concerns that we need to consider, or which might be problematic in the design of your project? You will need to discuss the answers to these questions with your supervisor as early as possible, so that your supervisor can ensure that your ideas are appropriate and feasible within the scope of the module, and so that you can progress with your plans independently following this discussion with your supervisor.

EMPLOYABILITY TIP!

First impressions count – make the most of this opportunity to make a good first impression by investing time in preparing for your initial meeting with your supervisor. Showing that you have planned ahead and thought about your project demonstrates planning, willingness and independent thought, which are all important for the dissertation module, but are also key employability skills!

2.5.2 Keeping a supervision record

It isn't just your initial meeting that you should prepare for – to get the most out of your supervision experience, you should come to all supervisory meetings with pre-prepared ideas and questions. It is important to be proactive and take responsibility for arranging supervisory meetings, making notes and following up on your meetings by responding to the feedback received. You should keep a record of what you have discussed with your supervisor, what actions you need to take in order to follow up on the points discussed, and what the aims are for the next meeting. One way of keeping these notes consistent is to use a supervision log, such as that depicted in Figure 2.1.

Meeting date:		
Issues discussed	Advice given	Action to be taken
Signature of student:	Signature of supervisor:	
Next meeting date:	Things to discuss at next meeting:	

Figure 2.1   Supervision log

EMPLOYABILITY TIP!

Come prepared to supervisory meetings with notes and questions to ask; keep notes during meetings on the points discussed and note action points to follow up on after each meeting. Being able to keep effective notes is an important employability skill that demonstrates your ability to prepare and manage your own work.

Summary

Managing the relationship with your supervisor on a practical level

You need to be able to manage the relationship with your supervisor practically throughout the module. This will include using your initiative and taking responsibility for the following tasks:

- Keeping regular contact and good communication with your supervisor
- Arranging regular supervision meetings and keeping your supervisor up to date with your progress and any issues you might have
- Keeping notes and following up on feedback

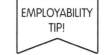

The supervisory relationship is key for developing important employability skills, such as working with others, building professional working relationships in the workplace, and written and verbal communication skills.

Chapter summary

In this chapter, we have discussed what it means to be 'independent' in your work, the importance of building a professional working relationship with your supervisor and how to manage the student–supervisor relationship. We have considered how processes of allocation to supervisors and the supervisory dynamic might differ between departments and institutions, and the importance of appreciating and discussing the individual supervisory style of your supervisor and your department. We have emphasised the importance of careful planning and note-taking, and how to manage meetings with your supervisor, and we have addressed some common concerns and questions that students have with their supervision, and how to tackle them professionally.

In the next few chapters, we will discuss how to make a start with your project ideas, and it is important that you discuss these ideas with your supervisor as they progress, in order to ensure that your project is both appropriate and feasible within the dissertation module.

Checklist

✓ Arrange to meet with your supervisor to discuss your initial project ideas.

✓ Plan and prepare for your initial meeting by conducting some reading around the topic area and making a list of questions to ask at your initial meeting.

✓ At your first meeting, discuss the following with your supervisor:

   o The supervision style of your supervisor;

   o Their expectations of you, and your expectations of them;

   o How to use your supervision time most effectively;

   o Key milestones and plans to submit draft sections for formative feedback;

   o Your topic choice, potential research questions and methodologies.

✓ Follow up on your meeting by writing up your notes and taking action on the points discussed.

✓ Get some dates in your diary for formative sections, key milestones and supervisory meetings.

3

Choosing a Research Topic

The ultimate aim of research, whether part of a student project or conducted by an academic member of staff or professional researcher, is to make a meaningful contribution to knowledge in the specified topic area. The first step in designing any research project is to identify what it is that you want to investigate. This chapter will guide you through the process of choosing a topic for your dissertation that is both *worthwhile* and *achievable* within the scope of your dissertation module.

Learning outcomes

By the end of this chapter you will:

- Be aware of methods that will help you to identify a topic for your dissertation
- Be able to consider what is feasible within the scope of your dissertation module.

3.1 Methods to help identify a topic

The first step in designing your dissertation project is to decide on a topic area to focus on. In this section, we explore some methods for identifying a suitable topic for your project.

3.1.1 Narrowing your focus: What interests you?

Narrowing your focus to a specific topic or research question can often seem quite a difficult task – particularly as you have covered so many different areas of psychology in your studies to date. Your first step in deciding on a topic should be to consider which areas you have found most interesting on your course so far. Being interested in your topic is key to success – if you're interested in something, you're more likely to enjoy studying it and it will motivate you to work on it.

Top tip!

Choosing a topic that interests you means that you are more likely to keep motivated throughout the processes of designing, conducting and writing up your dissertation project. Remember that you will be studying for your dissertation at the same time as completing other modules – so outside of your timetabled lectures and seminars, you will need to be motivated enough to want to spend your independent study time reading papers, planning your project, collecting your data and writing your dissertation.

3.1.2 Revisiting course material

Start by revisiting your past course material, one module or topic at a time. Think about whether there are any unanswered questions or unresolved issues within these topics that could warrant further research, or if there is something that really captured your attention and made you want to find out more. Focusing on something that interests you can be the key to motivation in your dissertation – and this will link to success. Read back over lecture notes, key reading material and your own notes to identify relevant points for exploration – there might be reference to a theory or existing findings that make you question something or wonder whether it could be applied to a different population. In turn, this process can help you to identify gaps in existing literature and knowledge, which might formulate a basis for your own research project.

3.1.3 Exploring the expertise of your lecturers

As discussed in Chapter 2, you will most likely be allocated to a supervisor from your department who will guide you throughout the dissertation process on a one-to-one basis. We've already mentioned how important it is that you choose a topic you are interested in, but it is also important that you capture the attention of your readers too, and one way of ensuring that you capture the interest of your supervisor is to explore their own areas of expertise. Start by reviewing staff profiles on your university webpage or in your course guides for an over-view of their interests, and follow by reading some of their publications for a deeper insight into their research. These steps may raise points for discussion with your supervisor, which could suggest potential research questions for your own project. Depending on the supervision practices within your department or institution, your supervisor might stipulate the topic and/or research methodology for your dissertation, so it is important to consider the compatibilities between your own interests and your supervisor's expertise. Refer back to Chapter 2 for further advice on this relationship.

Most departments will run research seminars throughout the academic year, so consider attending these to gain a deeper insight into the research being con-ducted in the wider department. It is a good idea to start doing this in advance of your dissertation module, as this can help you to prepare your ideas. Look out for presentations representing a range of psychological research topics and research methods – this will help you to develop multidisciplinary thinking (a good employability skill!), but also develops confidence in discussing and critiquing research, which will be beneficial to you when you start to write your literature review. Attending these events can provide you with a valuable insight into potential project topics, designs and methodologies. Showing willingness to attend these sessions also impresses potential supervisors and gives you a chance to talk to them about their research and gain experience of networking in a similar way to academic conferences.

> **EMPLOYABILITY TIP!**
>
> Attend your department's research seminars for a chance to develop your multidisciplinary thinking, critical discussion and networking skills. You'll learn about current research in your department as well as having an opportunity to speak to researchers directly about their projects.

3.1.4 Current affairs and 'hot topics'

There might be a particular issue in the news, media or politics at the time you are designing your study that raises potential research questions, or recent develop-ments in an area of interest which could provide a focal point for investigation. Typical examples are Brexit, police cuts, knife crime, terrorism, mental health in education, and various health epidemics, which have all sparked a recent interest from psychological researchers. One thing that you will need to consider when designing your study is the practical applications of potential findings – what contribution could your project make to knowledge in this area, and what impact could your research have in the real world? Focusing on a current issue in the news, media or society means that you have an obvious practical application in terms of informing knowledge, policy and practice. Think about issues in the news and whether there are any gaps in our knowledge in explaining a particular behaviour, phenomenon or outcome. If you do decide to go down this route of selecting a so-called 'hot topic', an important thing to be mindful of is that you are conducting a *psychology* dissertation, so you will need to look at such phenomena from a psychological perspective and apply psychological theory to help you explain it.

You can also identify hot topics by keeping up to date with psychological publications and social media accounts. It goes without saying that reading journal papers is one of the best ways to immerse yourself in existing research, but there are other ways of keeping up to date as well. Viewing conference proceedings can give you an insight into current research which may not yet be published, providing up-to-date information on current research findings and developments. Additionally, psychologists' blog sites, such as the BPS researcher digest and social media pages are good sources of topical discussions and can give you an insight into their viewpoints and ongoing research developments. Consider these as points for reflection – if you find something that interests you, reflect on what researchers have identified still needs to be done. This could form a basis for your own project.

3.1.5 Study replications

As you are reading through your course notes, you'll probably come across a multitude of classic theories which are most probably outdated – for example, Jean Piaget's conservation tasks, which were highly criticised for being too difficult for child participants to understand. You might find yourself questioning these theories and wondering whether a replication in the modern world would present different findings. There is value in replication, and it should not be overlooked as an important type of scientific research. Indeed, research must be replicated a number of times before we can accept the findings as a reliable and true representation. Over time or across different groups, findings may differ, even if the experimental conditions and methodology remain the same, so replications allow researchers to test theories about variables, relationships and effects.

Alternatively, you might consider whether an adaptation of an existing study would increase applicability to the modern world. Perhaps you could adapt an existing task for use in your own project. Alternatively, you may come across theories that were only tested in a very specific population, and you may find yourself wondering whether such a theory could be applied to a different population or subgroup. Replicating existing studies in new populations is popular amongst dissertation students, but remember that you need to be able to justify your decisions – so think about *why* you are doing this – why do we need to know whether a theory or finding also applies to a different population? What impact could this have?

3.1.6 Personal experiences

Often, our ideas are rooted in our own experiences. We are more likely to be interested in something that affects us or relates to our own lives. You may have experience of working in a particular area through volunteering or your part-time job, which might give you access to an otherwise difficult-to-access population. You may have a family member or friend with a physical or mental disability or learning difficulty, which may have sparked an interest in researching this further. You may have experienced a situation in your own life that has made you question a particular theory or existing protocol, or simply made you want to find out more or want to help people in the same situation. Utilising contacts from your personal life can provide you with access to participants in specific fields, and building upon your interests from your own experiences can provide valuable findings that can be applied to enhance knowledge and have implications for practice in the real world. Be cautious though – adopting a topic that is too 'close to home' has the potential to be damaging for your own mental health. For example, it would be advisable to avoid projects investigating depression if you suffer from mental health difficulties yourself. An important part of ethical approval is considering the impact that the research could have on you as a researcher; you need to protect yourself as well as your participants.

Top tip!

Be careful not to get too carried away or design a project that is too ambitious. As researchers, we have a tendency to want to change the world – but in reality, that's probably not going to be possible within the scope of a dissertation.

3.1.7 Links to your future career

In line with building on your interests, you might choose to conduct a dissertation project which has links to your future career aspirations. When you are applying for graduate jobs or postgraduate study, you will probably be asked about your dissertation – what did you do it on, and what did you learn? As well as discussing the transferable skills that you have developed throughout your degree, it's a great talking point if you can share some of your research findings with people who work in the field or who can relate to your research project. Perhaps you might be interested in going on to study a master's degree or to enrol on a training programme in an applied area of psychology – conducting your dissertation in a related field is a great way of kick-starting your experience of working and researching in this area.

Like many students, you might not know exactly what you want to do in the future, but you should be aware of how your dissertation could influence your path in life. As an academic now, I (Emily Harrison) often reflect on my own dissertation experience: I am a classic example of how your dissertation can open doors to your future career. When I was an undergraduate student, I chose to conduct my dissertation in the area of reading development as I had always been fascinated by how children learn to read. After discussing my interests with my supervisor, I conducted my dissertation investigating the relationship between children's sensitivity to the rhythm of spoken language and various literacy skills. I loved my dissertation from start to finish, and afterwards I was lucky enough to be offered a studentship to complete my PhD in a related area. Doing my PhD gave me other opportunities to engage in teaching at undergraduate level, which I'd never considered before, and I loved it! I've never looked back since, and I have my dissertation supervisor to thank for where I am now – I certainly wouldn't be writing this book if my experience had been different!

Top tip!

Take time to consider your ideas, discuss them with your supervisor and consider what opportunities your dissertation could create for your future.

Homework

We've presented a range of methods above that can help you to identify a topic for your dissertation. Create a spider diagram for each method, and then look for common links between them - is there something that links your interests to your supervisor's expertise and your future career aspirations?

3.2 Original versus worthwhile

Whilst it is important to choose a topic that interests you, your research topic also needs to be something that is meaningful and worthwhile researching. Creating originality in your design is one way of producing new findings that make a unique contribution to knowledge – to do this you will need to identify a gap – we'll talk more about this in Chapter 4. But remember, just because there is an apparent gap in current research or knowledge, it doesn't necessarily mean that this is something that needs to be researched – or even *can* be researched, particularly within the scope of a dissertation. As you develop your rationale, you need to think about the reasons *why* you have chosen to design this particular project – and simply saying that it hasn't been done before is unfortunately not sufficient. You will need to argue the case for why your project is needed. It's not just about what we don't know about a topic, it's also about why we need to know more – why is it worthwhile? A replication can still answer this question, as it is always worthwhile double-checking research findings – it is not necessary for your study to be completely original in its design.

Top tip!

Research is about making a meaningful contribution to Knowledge – consider why we need to Know this; justification is Key.

3.3 What is feasible?

As mentioned in Chapter 1, most departments will be fairly flexible in allowing you to conduct your dissertation in almost any area of psychology. This is obviously subject to ethical approval and access to participants, so you may need to consider an alternative design in order to meet ethical requirements. Your university ethics committee will have a duty of care towards you as a student and will need to ensure that you are protected from physical and psychological harm in the same way that you must protect your participants. As such, it's unlikely that you would be permitted to work with offenders or to collect data in a dangerous environment. You also need to consider what is possible within the scope and time frame of an undergraduate dissertation. It's common for students interested in health psychology to want to work with the NHS, but for this you would also need to gain NHS ethical approval, which can be a lengthy process. For this reason, we would discourage students from pursuing projects with these populations at undergraduate level, and to think about alternative ways of exploring your chosen topic area. For example, rather than working with offenders, you could explore people's perceptions of offenders; or rather than working with terminally ill patients, you could explore the experiences of family members or people working in close proximity to these patients.

As well as considering what is possible in terms of access to participants, it is also important to consider what is realistic in terms of your design within the time frame of your dissertation module. Don't overcomplicate things – students have a tendency to be overly ambitious with project design and we often have to remind them that the dissertation needs to be completed within a few months and in just a single study! A simple design allows you more room to explore your theoretical perspective, develop a stronger rationale, clearly explain your design and explore your findings in more detail. This can often reward you with a higher mark than if you try to cram in too many research questions or variables, and you can always discuss your other ideas in the section on 'directions for future research' in your discussion chapter.

Top tip!

Don't overcomplicate things – sometimes a simpler design will reward you with a higher mark as it allows you more time and space to explore your theoretical perspective, justify your decisions and explain your findings in detail.

3.4 What makes a good project idea?

So, taking all of the above into consideration, what makes a good project idea? Well, it's a little like building a house. Firstly, it needs to have strong foundations – it needs to be rooted in psychological literature. It needs to be strong – to stand up to criticism, to have a strong rationale. It needs to have a selling point – something that makes a meaningful contribution to knowledge. It needs to be realistic and achievable – something that you can manage within the scope of your dissertation module. And to complete it, you'll need specialist knowledge and skills – so it needs to be something that you have a clear understanding of.

Consider what skills you already have that you can utilise in your dissertation – what do you have a clear understanding of? You might recall a particular lecture or topic that you enjoyed because you understood it better than others. This might be a useful starting point for you. Consider research methodology as well as the topic – what methods do you understand better than others? What are you good at? Look back at your marks and feedback for your coursework in your other modules and consider what you have done well at so far. Whilst there needs to be a clear link between your research question and your methodology, don't be afraid to play to your strengths.

Top tip!

> Ask yourself not just what you are interested in, but also what you are good at, and what you have a clear understanding of. Play to your strengths and you are likely to succeed.

Generally, a good project idea is one that has been well thought out, one that has a strong rationale and one that makes a clear contribution to knowledge. Below are some common pitfalls that we have observed with student projects in the past, to give you an idea of what to avoid.

Common pitfalls

- Having your heart set on researching a particular phenomenon and later finding that access to participants is too difficult or time-consuming for your dissertation
- Deciding on a topic or research question without taking the time to research it fully and later discovering that there is little to no psychological literature related to it and/or no clear rationale for studying it
- Deciding on a topic or research question based on your lecture notes or textbooks without reading recent journal articles. If you start to design your study without reading recent journal articles, you run the risk of later discovering that your project idea has already been done
- Deciding on a research design that is unlikely to gain ethical approval. If your ethics application gets rejected, you will have no choice but to change your design, losing valuable research time in doing so. You are already on a tight timescale with your dissertation module, so you can't afford to keep going backwards and forwards with ethics. For this reason, it is really important that you understand the ethical requirements from the beginning, and that you discuss your ideas with your supervisor as soon as possible
- Including too many research questions and/or variables in your design, making your study too complex and running the risk of running out of time and/or not being able to address everything in sufficient detail.

Chapter summary

- In this chapter, we have discussed ways of identifying a suitable research topic: by considering your interests, revisiting course material, exploring the expertise of your lecturers, considering current 'hot topics', considering study replications, thinking about your personal experiences and your future career aspirations.
- We have discussed what makes a good project: something worthwhile, not overly ambitious, and feasible within the scope of your dissertation module.

Checklist

✓ Work through the sections of this chapter and consider your ideas in relation to each method of selecting a topic.

✓ If you have not done so already, book an appointment with your supervisor to talk through your ideas and what is feasible within the scope of your dissertation module.

4

Understanding the Literature

This chapter will guide you through the process of exploring and understanding existing literature. This chapter will provide guidance on how to find relevant journal papers, how to read a journal article, how to make useful notes and how to report existing findings in your literature review. We will discuss how to structure your literature review and the importance of being able to formulate a strong argument within your writing.

Learning outcomes

By the end of this chapter you will:

- Understand some principles of how to conduct an effective literature search
- Understand how to read a journal article and make effective notes
- Understand how to structure your literature review chapter.

4.1 Exploring existing literature

By the time you read this section you will, we hope, have an idea of the topic that you want to focus on for your dissertation, but there is still a long way to go in developing your chosen topic into a research project. Once you have decided on a topic area, the next step in narrowing your focus is to search through the literature to determine what research already exists in this area – what has already been done, and what do we already know? Searching through the literature in this way is known as a 'literature search', and in doing so, you are aiming to identify a more specific research area that could potentially be addressed by your project. By ensuring that your project extends or responds to existing research in the field, you will ensure that your project is rooted in psychological literature.

4.1.1 Developing background knowledge

At this stage in your degree, you would be correct in thinking that you should be focusing your reading on primary sources of information, such as journal articles, rather than sourcing information from textbooks and other secondary sources. Textbooks often reproduce information regarding research findings, which can cause misunderstandings or inaccuracies – in other words, it is best to get your information straight from the horse's mouth and go direct to the original papers where possible. Whilst this is generally true, students often mistake this as meaning that you can't use textbooks – wrong! If you're exploring an area that hasn't been covered in detail on your course, the chances are that you won't have the relevant background knowledge you need to understand the journal articles to a sufficient standard. As a result, students often complain that they struggle to understand journal papers.

The most effective way of gaining a general understanding of a topic area is to conduct some background reading using good quality textbooks. Take a trip to your university library and see what you can find on your chosen topic area. Don't forget to make some notes as you go along, as they will form the basis of your understanding of the topic. Reading textbooks is a great way of exploring key terminology, classic theories and key studies in your chosen area, and helps you build up a general understanding of the topic and what we already know. For example, if you wish to explore the topic of childhood attachment, start by searching for textbooks on early childhood development and look for chapters on attachment theory. Textbooks will also give you a general indication of so-called 'big names' in the area – people whose research you might want to look up later when you begin exploring journal articles and research findings in more depth.

Top tip!

> Be sure to write down references to papers as you read about them in textbooks so that you can look up the original papers later.

4.1.2 Literature searching

From your exploration of textbooks in the area, you should have generated a list of researchers in the area and potential papers to read. The first step in exploring the literature in more depth is to locate as many of these papers as possible in their primary form, and to explore the further work of the big names in your chosen area. As you do so, you will notice that authors will reference other papers by researchers in the same area, which you might also want to look up in their primary form. This will create a bit of a snowball effect, where you can use one paper to find references to other papers, and so on, until you have built up a picture of what we already know in your chosen topic area. In order to find these papers in their original form, as well as other relevant papers, you will need to use literature searching databases, such as Science Direct, Scopus, PsycInfo and Google Scholar.

Your university will have a subscription to a number of psychological and scientific journals via their online platforms, and you should have had plenty of experience in using these literature-searching databases throughout the course of your studies to date. If you need assistance in using these platforms, contact your subject librarian. In the next section of this chapter, we will provide some tips on how to find relevant journal papers to help you locate relevant research findings to guide the development of your project.

4.1.2.1 How to find relevant journal papers

At the beginning of your literature-searching journey, you would be forgiven for feeling a little overwhelmed by the vastness of your literature searches and the sheer number of articles that greet you. Without being able to minimise the results of your literature search effectively, you run the risk of getting lost. The key to a successful literature search is being able to identify the most appropriate and relevant papers to read further, minimising unnecessary work. One way of doing this is to use an 'advanced search' option, which will allow you to specify further details about the types of articles you wish to find. For example, you can specify multiple search terms, choose a period of publication, specify author names or select a specific journal. The more specific you can be in your search, the more manageable and applicable your search results will be. If your advanced search returns too few papers, you'll need to go back and broaden your search parameters.

Start with one term for your topic area and think about alternative terms that relate to the same topic – you can use a thesaurus if you need to. Make a list of these terms and consider how they relate to one another – you can create a mind map if you wish. Replicate your search several times, alternating your combination of search terms to fully explore the existing papers in the area. As you do so, continue to make a note of any papers that you want to read in full, and save the full-text versions if you can. Try to avoid getting drawn into papers that sound interesting but are not clearly related to the topic you are wanting to research. This will cause you to go off at a tangent and get lost in the wider literature. It's also a good idea to focus on contemporary research articles, published within the last ten years, as research findings can quickly become outdated as new research is published. That is not to say you should discard any papers that are more than ten years old, but you should be mindful that claims you make in relation to the findings of older papers will need to be supported with more contemporary findings in order for them to be valid in the context of your developing research project.

Homework

Create a mind map of key terms in your chosen topic area. Alternate your use of key term combinations throughout your literature search to identify all the relevant papers for your literature review. As you do so, be sure to make a note of the references of these papers – you'll need these later and writing them down now will save you time in the long run!

Through your various searches, you can begin to identify relevant papers by their titles or by authors whose names you recognise from your background reading. Some papers can be eliminated immediately by their titles; for others, you will need to read the abstract. An abstract will usually give an overview of the methodology and findings of a paper, so you can identify whether it is relevant to your chosen topic or whether it is too far removed from your area of focus. As you work through your list of papers reading the abstracts, you will be able to eliminate further papers from your reading list and identify those that will be of benefit to your developing literature review. As you read the abstracts, ask yourself the following questions to help you identify their significance:

- Is the area relevant to the topic you want your dissertation to focus on?
- Is the focus of the article broadly or more specifically related to your topic?
- What methods were used in this study, and could they be applied to your own study in some way?
- What were the findings of this study? How do they help you to understand the topic area? How might these findings help to create a research question for your own study?
- Are there any obvious limitations to this study that could be overcome in future research?

EMPLOYABILITY
TIP!

Routinely asking yourself the above questions as you search for relevant literature will help you to practise your critical thinking skills – a key employability skill, but it will also help you to narrow down your search and collate key information to use in your literature review.

Your next step will be to read the full text of the most relevant papers in depth. In the next section, we discuss how to read a journal article effectively.

4.1.2.2 How to read a journal article

At this stage, you may be wondering *how* to go about reading a journal paper effectively. The first thing you should note is that journal papers follow a very similar format to the research reports that you will be used to writing as part of your coursework, and are shorter versions of the one you will produce for your dissertation. Empirical journal papers will contain an overview of existing literature, a methodology section, details of data analysis and results, and a discussion of the findings. In order to gain a deep level of understanding of each article, you will need to read it multiple times – so it is absolutely fine to skim it the first time round. You should pay attention to the discussion section first, working backwards. The discussion will provide you with an overview of the key findings and conclusions of the study – further allowing you to evaluate the relevance of the paper to your own project ideas. The findings will be reported in more detail in the results section, but the discussion will most likely summarise these findings in a simpler way, allowing you to grasp the key message of the article. In addition, many journal articles will identify directions for future research towards the end of the discussion section, so this is something you should look out for – it may give you an idea of where the gaps are in existing research, and what still needs to be done. Be careful when reading dated articles though – if you focus on the conclusions of older papers, the chances are that any gaps identified here may have already been filled by the time you come to design your own study.

Caution!

Be wary of focusing too much attention on articles more than ten years old. The chances are that if you design your study based on an older paper, your study may have already been done in the time between then and now. Designing your study to fill a gap or future direction that was identified ten years ago may result in a lack of meaningful contribution.

Once you have identified the key findings, the next section to read is the methodology. As you read through to the method section of papers, you should note the different designs that are reported in research papers in your topic area. Reading existing papers can give you an idea of the possible designs that you could employ or adapt for your own study, and the materials and measures that have been used to assess particular variables in the specified field, which you may want to utilise yourself. You should also pay attention to the sample of participants – this will give you an idea of which population the results of the study apply to, and whether the findings can be generalised more widely. There might be an opportunity to create a replication of a particular study with a different population (see section 3.1.5).

It might sound odd to start off by reading a paper backwards, but this means that by the time you get to the literature review, you have already gained an idea of the findings, conclusions and suggested future directions listed within the paper (which might all lead to a research question for your project). If you still think this study is relevant to the development of your own project, the literature review is important because it gives you an insight into the background literature that led to this particular study. You may want to use some of this knowledge in the development of your own literature review – it may provide you with additional references for papers that may also be relevant to your project, so it's important to take note of key papers that are discussed. Pay attention to the way other authors discuss the literature, too – the terminology they use may give you an indication of other terms that could be used in your literature search to identify additional, potentially more recent papers than the one you are reading. Remember, if you're reading a paper published in any given year, the actual research was probably conducted two or more years prior to the publication date, so there are likely to have been further developments in the research area since.

After you've read a paper the first time, you will have a general understanding of the arguments. You'll need to re-read it a few times to develop a deeper level of critical evaluation – this is important for the development of your critical analysis skills, which will need to be communicated in your literature review, so don't put off re-reading the same papers again.

> EMPLOYABILITY TIP!

Reading and re-reading papers will help you to develop your critical thinking skills and your basic understanding of an article into a critical understanding – something that will need to be communicated in your literature review and throughout your dissertation. Critical thinking is also a key transferable skill that will be relevant to the job market.

4.1.2.3 How to make useful notes

For each paper you read, you'll need to make a note of the following information:

- **The full reference for the paper (in APA format)**: It is important for you to be able to find the article again later, and also for your reference list. Trust us, it will save you time later!
- **The research question/aims**: Looking back at these notes will help you to quickly identify the questions that have already been addressed by the literature.
- **The design and variables**: These will help you to collate information on the different designs and variables studied in previous research.
- **The population being studied**: As above, this will help you to collate information on the samples of participants that have previously been studied. You may notice that particular designs consistently tend to recruit participants from similar populations, which may present you with potential gaps to address.
- **The key findings**: They are important for your understanding of what is already known about the area.
- **The conclusions**: They are important for your general understanding of existing knowledge in your chosen topic area, and potential directions for future research. As mentioned earlier, there may have been further developments in knowledge since some of the papers were published, so seeing all of the conclusions in one place will allow you to see what has been achieved and where gaps still remain.

Refer to our **online resources** for a useful table that you can populate with this information for each paper you read. As you read more and more papers and record your notes, you will begin to notice links between different studies. You will be able to start mapping the literature to visualise how knowledge in the topic area has developed over time, and this will provide the backbone for your literature review chapter.

Homework

Complete the research papers table with your findings from your literature search. This will be a useful document to refer back to as you begin to write up your literature review.

4.2 Structuring your literature review chapter

From completing the task in the section above, you should have an idea of what research findings you want to discuss within your literature review, and what story you want to tell. Your literature review should organise the discussion of literature into key points, with each point becoming a paragraph. Each paragraph should discuss one point and lead clearly into the next paragraph in order to generate flow within your writing. Overly long or underdeveloped paragraphs demonstrate a lack of clear thinking and in-depth analysis of points, so try to maintain a balance between conciseness and sufficient discussion of information.

Even once you've broken the literature down into manageable chunks, it can often be difficult to structure the discussion effectively. One of the best ways to create a strong argument within your literature review is to think about the shape and story of the discussion – tell the story by creating an 'egg timer' shape to your dissertation (Figure 4.1). The top half of the egg timer represents the literature review, starting off with a broad overview of the topic area. Here, you can use the knowledge you have developed from reading textbooks and more generic papers on your wider topic area. As you progress through your literature review, you will progressively narrow your focus until you reach a point where you have identified a specific gap in the literature or specific question that you are then going to explore in your own study. Your study forms the 'sand' in the egg timer, filling the gap in existing knowledge. But, in order to allow the sand to pass through the egg timer, you first need to identify the rationale for doing so, and the methods you will use. This will be explored further in the following chapters.

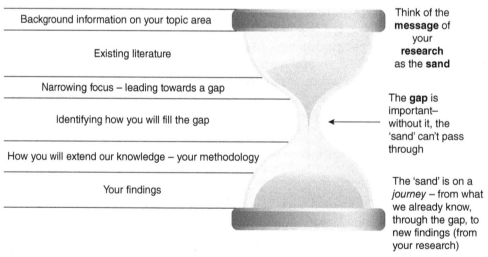

Figure 4.1 The 'egg timer'

4.2.1 Introducing and creating links between papers

You can introduce a paper in two main ways: either (1) start by introducing the author(s), and follow with an overview of their work – for example, 'Harrison, Wood, Holliman and Vousden (2018) investigated the effectiveness of a rhythmic based reading intervention in beginning readers and found that...', or (2) start by introducing the paper, and follow by citing the author(s) – for example, 'Training children on rhythmic awareness has been shown to be effective for improving reading skills (Harrison, Wood, Holliman & Vousden, 2018)'. You will also need to think about how to create links between the papers you discuss. The best way to do this is to think about the story you are telling and group the papers into sections of the story. Do papers explain the general topic area, or do they report more specific research relevant to what you aim to do in your own study? For example, in the paper mentioned above, the authors begin by discussing factors that influence reading development in general and then narrow the focus to the role of rhythmic awareness, later discussing existing intervention studies, and finally identifying a gap in existing knowledge, leading to their own study. In a similar way, you might begin by identifying the wider topic area, narrow your focus to the relationship or phenomenon you are looking at in your own study, then discuss key papers relevant to your own project, and finally identify the gap in existing knowledge that you plan to address.

If you wish to, you can use subheadings to group the discussion of papers into larger sections. Using subheadings in this way will help to create more manageable subsections for your reader and can be a useful way of aiding the development of your argument. Subheadings can be particularly useful if you have more than one research question and/or hypothesis, helping to break your discussion of the literature into sections that demonstrate your understanding of the different strands of your research topic. The important thing to consider is whether or not subheadings benefit the discussion of information and the formation of your argument. As a rule of thumb, each paragraph should usually only communicate one main point, so think about the points you want to make, and organise them in a way that tells the story you want to tell, one point per paragraph, with paragraphs grouped into sections of your story, as discussed above.

4.2.2 Paragraph structure

Generally, it is not good academic practice to start a paragraph with a reference, so consider this when structuring your paragraphs and sentences. So, rather than beginning with 'Name (2008) found that X is related to Y', begin by making a point and then evidence that point by referring to research – for example, 'X has been shown to be related to Y. Name (2008) found that…'. Once you've made your point and provided evidence to support your claim, consider how you will create a link between this and the next point you wish to make.

One way of ensuring that your paragraphs follow a clear structure is to start each paragraph with a topic sentence. This is a sentence which signposts the reader to the content of the paragraph. Importantly, however, each paragraph should also link clearly to the preceding paragraph, to form a logical discussion, so in some cases it might not be appropriate to use a topic sentence at the beginning of a paragraph. A common pitfall we see in literature reviews is that many students struggle to make links between their paragraphs and between the discussion of different papers they have read and written about in the literature review. This often results in a list-like discussion, with no clear links between each paper. Try not to start paragraphs repeatedly with list-like statements such as 'Another study…', 'Additionally' and 'Furthermore', and instead try to be more creative with your language to formulate a more sophisticated discussion of the literature. Organising the discussion of research papers logically and implementing effective transitions between paragraphs will help your reader to understand the argument you are trying to make. Even very short transitions between points can be very effective – for example, using 'consequently' or 'as a result' to lead to a subsequent point can help to formulate a logical story for your reader. Paying careful attention to paragraph structure and links between paragraphs will demonstrate a more thorough understanding of the literature and will also strengthen your argument and demonstrate better academic writing skills. Importantly, it will create flow in your writing – something which your examiners will be looking for.

4.2.3 Formulating a critical discussion

Throughout your literature review, you need to be formulating a critical discussion of research evidence in order to form a strong argument. In order to do this, you need to think critically about the studies you are reporting: What have they done well? And what could be improved? Are their arguments valid? Was their design appropriate? Were there any methodological limitations? What is their theoretical perspective, and is it well supported within their paper? How could we improve this study if we were to replicate it? You will need to communicate your answers to some of these questions within your literature review. By identifying some of the downfalls of one paper, you can lead in to the discussion of other papers (e.g. has other research been conducted since which has addressed some of these downfalls?), revealing the story of how literature in this topic area has developed over time and how our knowledge to date has been shaped by existing research. In doing so, you will formulate a chronological critical discussion, leading smoothly to the identification of your own research question(s), which we will explore in more detail in Chapter 5.

Top tip!

Being able to formulate a strong argument relies on two main things:

- Effective structure, and
- Critical analysis.

Critical analysis is an important employability skill. Being able to demonstrate your ability to think critically about situations, research methodologies and findings within your literature review will help to build a strong argument in your dissertation. Being able to formulate a strong argument is another important transferable skill.

Chapter summary

In this chapter, we have considered how to conduct an effective literature search, how to read a journal article to extract key information and how to report the results of your literature search in your literature review chapter effectively. This chapter has also covered how to structure your literature review to formulate a strong argument within your writing effectively. Being able to form a strong argument is imperative for the clarity and strength of your rationale.

Checklist

✓   Make a list of search terms to use during your literature search.

✓   Use literature searching databases to locate and make a note of relevant papers.

✓   Complete the literature review table to note important information about each paper.

✓   Make a note of the full references of relevant papers so that you can find them later on.

✓   Start thinking about the story you want to tell in your literature review and how you can structure the discussion of literature effectively.

4.3 Next steps

Now that you've got an idea of what has already been done and what we already know about your topic, the next step is to develop a strong rationale for your project. You should consider what your aims/research question(s) might be. In the next chapter, we will explore how to develop a strong rationale (justification) for your project aims, and how to identify a suitable research question.

5

Developing Your Rationale, Research Question(s) and Hypothesis; and Choosing between Quantitative and Qualitative Research Design

Developing a strong rationale for your project is imperative for the clear communication of your aims. The rationale is where you explain the reasons *why* you are doing what you are doing, and why it is so important. This leads in to your research question(s), and if you are planning a quantitative project it will also link to your hypothesis. This chapter will guide you through the process of developing a strong, clear rationale and producing well-justified research questions for your project.

Learning outcomes

By the end of this chapter you will:

- Understand the importance of a strong rationale and how it maps on to the rest of your project
- Be able to formulate a research question and understand how it maps on to the choice of research design
- Be able to justify your decisions over your research design based on your research question and aims.

5.1 The importance of a strong rationale

As mentioned earlier, the rationale for your study needs to be rooted in psychological literature, so your literature review should be structured in a way that tells a story (see the 'egg timer' in section 4.2). As you begin to narrow your focus in the literature review, your discussion of existing research should naturally lead towards the identification of a gap in existing knowledge. You can be creative here and lead your study in any direction you choose by carefully selecting literature that leads your discussion to identify a specific gap (as there may be many gaps or multiple opportunities for different studies). Your aim will then be to address this gap in some way with your study. Your rationale should build on this – the key here is *justification*. The most important part of writing a dissertation is that you are able to justify every decision you have made throughout the process – and this all builds on your rationale. Keep asking yourself, 'Why?' after every decision and make sure you have an answer. Here are a few questions to ask yourself now:

- What question(s) remain unanswered by existing literature?
- Why is it important that you fill the gap you have identified?
- What can you tell us that we didn't know before?
- What impact could your findings have in the real world?
- *How* can you fill this gap?

Top tip!

> The key to a strong rationale is to justify every decision you have made – with every decision, keep asking yourself, 'Why?' and make sure you have an answer embedded within your writing.

In considering the above questions, you will formulate a clearer idea of why you are doing what you are doing in your research. In particular, we will draw your attention to the importance of not only considering *what* you are planning to do but also *why* you are planning to do it. As mentioned earlier in this book, unfortunately it is not sufficient to find a gap in existing research and simply say, 'It's never been done before.' The question you really need to ask yourself here is, 'Why is it important that I do this? – What difference will it make? What will this tell us?' And, importantly, 'Why do we need to know this?' Clearly justifying the importance of your project at this stage will ensure that you have a clear understanding of the meaningful contribution that your project will make, and, as we discuss later in this chapter, your rationale will map on to *all* other sections of your dissertation, so a weak rationale will be evident throughout your work.

For example, say you were interested in conducting your research project on the relationship between people's eating habits and their reaction times. Consider the importance of determining this relationship – what might the practical application of the findings be? In this particular project, you could say that if there is a significant positive relationship between regularity of eating and the speed of a person's reaction times, those who need to have quick reactions, for example drivers, should be encouraged to eat at regular intervals. Why is it important that we investigate this relationship? Because if irregular eating has a negative effect on people's reaction times, this could result in accidents on the road. We should note here that in designing your study, it is important also to consider confounding variables or mediating variables that might play a role in a relationship like this, such as sleep/tiredness, mental state, physical health and environment factors, but we will discuss project design a little later.

Top tip!

> Justifying the importance of your project at this stage will ensure that you have a clear understanding of the meaningful contribution that your project will make. Consider not just what you plan to do but why it is important that you do it. A weak rationale will be evident throughout the chapters of your dissertation.

Your rationale justifies *why* you should focus on a particular topic, and this will lead to your research questions, which will be identified by considering *what* it is, specifically, that you want to find out.

EMPLOYABILITY TIP!

Paying attention to the importance of the *Why?* question, and being able to answer it, helps you to justify your decisions – an important transferable skill.

5.2 The research question(s)

The research question (or questions) you ask at the beginning of your dissertation will shape the entire project – it defines the purpose of this piece of research and is pivotal in guiding the development of your research methodology, the chosen data analysis strategy and the discussion of findings. The research question will usually appear at the end of the literature review, after you have discussed existing literature and come to a conclusion about what has already been done and what gaps remain in our current knowledge of your chosen topic area. You can have more than one research question if there is more than one thing that you hope to find out through conducting your project. This is common if you have a more complex design in mind with multiple (quantitative) variables, or you want to explore a complex topic (qualitatively) with your participants. Remember, you will need to show *how* you are going to answer each of these questions when it comes to planning the methodology of your dissertation, so try to keep your questions as simple as possible. For an undergraduate project, it is perfectly acceptable and somewhat expected that you will only have one research question that you aim to answer – so try not to overcomplicate things.

Top tip!

Try not to overcomplicate things when defining your research question(s). Keep each question simple and try not to give yourself too much to do within your project (one simple question is perfectly acceptable!). Remember, each question will need to be addressed separately within your methodology, and answers reported within your results chapter.

So, what should your research question *look like*? You may wish to test an existing theory by replicating or changing existing methodological designs or procedures, either with a similar or different sample of participants to an original study. If you wish to do this, think about what you want to find out – for example, 'Is there a relationship between X and Y in participants (from a particular population)?' You may want to evaluate the effectiveness of a particular method, treatment, intervention or technique on a specified outcome measure, or you may want to find out if an experimental condition affects participants' performance on a task more than a control condition. In this case, you might ask, 'Can X affect Y?' Or you may want to explore participants' views or opinions of a particular phenomenon qualitatively, so you might ask, 'What are participants' views about X?'.

There are certain types of questions that you should avoid, because these can cause difficult problems in research design and/or disrupt your rationale. We have outlined some of these questions to avoid below.

Questions to avoid

- Questions that aren't rooted in psychological literature: Remember that your question will govern the direction of your project – if it is not rooted in psychological literature, your rationale will be weak.
- Questions that aren't questions: Make sure you actually *ask* something.
- Questions that have already been answered: Remember that the point of research is to make a meaningful contribution to knowledge.
- Questions that can't be answered: Make sure you can realistically find an answer.
- Leading questions: Your prediction will come later – ask the question first, then make your prediction about the answer.
- Questions that indicate that you want to 'prove' something: Unfortunately, *prove* is a very strong word; we would suggest looking for *support* rather than proof.
- Questions that are too complicated: Make sure your question is simple enough to be answered with a single method of data collection and analysis. If you need to conduct multiple analyses to find an answer, your question should probably be broken down into multiple questions. If this is the case, ask yourself whether you *need* to answer all of this within a single study, or whether you are being too ambitious.
- Questions that require specialist equipment, resources or funding; questions that require participants who are difficult to access; or questions that would require longitudinal research to answer: Whilst these points don't necessarily make for a bad research question, they would be unreasonable for an undergraduate project.

In contrast to the examples above then, what is a *good* research question? A good research question is one that:

- Is rooted in psychological literature
- Allows you to address your research aim and rationale, and make a meaningful contribution to knowledge
- Is simple and easy to understand
- Is clearly testable, and has clear links to a defined methodology
- You can answer within the scope of your dissertation module.

EMPLOYABILITY TIP!

Being able to understand what is achievable and feasible is an important employability skill, as it shows that you can make effective use of your time and skills whilst also knowing your limits.

Importantly, you will next need to employ a methodological approach and data analysis strategy that are appropriate for answering your research question(s), so it is important to invest a significant amount of time in thinking about the development of your question, as this governs later decisions surrounding the design of your study.

5.3 Quantitative versus qualitative research

When deciding on a style of research, the most important thing is that you choose a design that maps on well to your research question. Unfortunately, research doesn't usually work well if you start with a design in mind – you need to start with the literature, identify a gap, decide on what you want to find out, and then design a study that can answer your research question. Once you've decided on a research question, sometimes you *will* have the option of deciding between qualitative or quantitative design, but you need to be prepared for the eventuality that your question just won't lend itself to the design you'd prefer to run. So, don't just think 'I hate stats' (many students think like this!), and remember that you will have support throughout your project, including data analysis, so don't be afraid to challenge yourself.

It is important to choose a design that best helps you to answer your research question. Most of the time, the link between your question and design will be clear-cut. If you are interested in finding out about the differences between two groups or the relationship between variables, then a quantitative design will suit your project best, and it wouldn't be logical to try to test this with a qualitative interview and thematic analysis. If you're more interested in the experiences or opinions of participants from a particular group, then a qualitative design would suit your project best.

Top tip!

> Choose a design that helps you to best answer your research question. Starting with a design in mind can be problematic, and it is important to understand the links between your research question and the appropriate methodology.

Sometimes your design options are not so obvious and some projects may lend themselves to both types of design – as mentioned above, in these cases you *will* have a choice over the direction in which you want to take your project. For example, if you are interested in the views of participants towards a minority group, you could measure this quantitatively using a Likert-type scale question-naire, or qualitatively through the use of interviews. The design you choose will determine which direction your project takes – in these cases, the finalisation of your research question and the design often go hand in hand, and you'll be able to tweak the wording of your question to suit your choice of design. For exam-ple, if you decide to go down the quantitative route, you could break your participants down into different age groups/genders and ask, 'Do participants' views of [group] differ depending on their age group/gender?'. Alternatively, if you choose to go down the qualitative route, you could ask, 'What are partici-pants' experiences of and views of [group]?'. In order to decide on the best methodology for your project, you will need to think about what it is that you most want to find out – are you more interested in the statistical evidence for a phenomenon or relationship, or are you more interested in participants' experi-ences of such a phenomenon? If you're stuck on deciding which route to go down, play to your strengths. What are you good at? Which types of assess-ment have you done best at in the past? Look back at the feedback you received for both quantitative and qualitative pieces of coursework that you have com-pleted earlier in your course to help you understand what your strengths are, where there is room for improvement and what your weaknesses are. Think about the type of work you most enjoy too, as this will affect your motivation. In Chapters 6 and 7, we will explore quantitative and qualitative methodology in more detail.

5.4 Hypotheses

If you're conducting quantitative research, the research question will be followed by a hypothesis, and you will usually have one hypothesis or prediction for each research question (i.e. you will predict the answer to each question you ask). You will not usually find a hypothesis in a qualitative project – a hypothesis is some-thing that can be *scientifically tested*, so it is usually found only in quantitative projects where a statistical analysis will provide a statistical answer to your question.

The hypothesis is a prediction about what you think the data will show – what do you think the answer to your question will be? You should think carefully about your hypothesis – as with the question, it should be rooted in psycho-logical literature and should be a logical prediction based on existing knowledge of the topic and the research findings that you have discussed in your literature review. At this stage, it is important to consider your theoretical standpoint with respect to your topic area. Your theoretical standpoint refers to your beliefs surrounding the topic (based on existing theory and related research, which should have already been discussed in the literature review) that under-pin your hypothesis. As with the rationale, return to that 'Why?' question – think

53

about *why* you have predicted a certain outcome. It would be useful if you could include a statement of explanation with your hypothesis, to show your examiner why you have predicted this – for example, 'Based on findings by Smith (2019), it is predicted that there will be a negative correlation between X and Y.'

Your hypothesis can be directional (i.e. predicting the direction of a relationship), for example predicting a positive or negative correlation between variables, or a higher or lower score on an outcome variable in one group compared to another. Alternatively, you can have a non-directional hypothesis (i.e. simply stating that there will be a relationship or correlation between variables, but not *what kind* of relationship). It is important to understand the impact your hypothesis can have on your results – if you make a directional hypothesis, you will need to conduct a one-tailed significance test in your data analysis, whereas, if you make a non-directional hypothesis, you will need to conduct a two-tailed significance test. We will talk more about this later in Chapter 10.

5.5 How it all fits together

As discussed throughout this and the previous chapters of this book, it is imperative that you understand, and are able to clearly communicate, the links between your rationale, research question(s) and chosen methodology. A handy flowchart that summarises these links is shown in Figure 5.1.

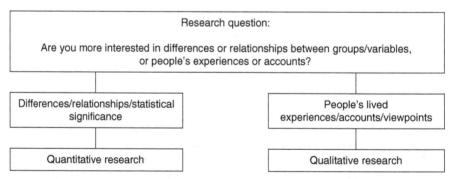

Figure 5.1   Flowchart demonstrating the links between research questions and quantitative/qualitative methodology

Homework

Work on strengthening your rationale by considering not just what you want to do, but also why it is important that you do this. Use the development of your rationale to help you phrase an appropriate research question for your study, and start to think about what methods might be most appropriate for helping you to answer this question.

Book an appointment with your supervisor to discuss your research question and methodology in more detail to ensure that these decisions are feasible and appropriate.

Chapter summary

- The key to a strong rationale is being able to justify every decision you have made during the dissertation process. In this chapter, we have discussed the importance of a strong rationale and how to ensure that your project is rooted in psychological literature.
- We have discussed how to formulate a research question and hypothesis, and how this dictates your choice of research design.

Checklist

✓ Use the information sourced in your literature review to help you form a rationale for your project.

✓ Decide on your research question.

✓ Decide what the most appropriate methodology might be to help you answer your research question.

METHODOLOGY

Devising an appropriate research methodology to help you address your research question

The most important question you can ask yourself at the beginning of your research design journey is, 'What type of methodology is most appropriate for addressing your research question?' By this point in your research design, you will (hopefully) have a good idea of what research already exists on your topic area, what gaps remain and what you want to find out next. This will have formed a research question and/or aim for your study. As discussed in Chapter 5, certain types of research question lend themselves better to a particular type of research design. For example, if you are interested in finding out about the difference between groups, or the relationship between variables, quantitative methodology will allow you to explore statistical comparisons or analyses of relationships. Furthermore, quantitative research methods are a good tool when you want to examine/manipulate your variables in controlled conditions. However, if you are more interested in finding out about participants' lived experiences of a particular event, or their opinions, or their attitudes towards a particular phenomenon, then qualitative methods may be better suited to helping you gain a more in-depth understanding of your participants' accounts. We will talk more about qualitative research methodology in Chapter 7, but, for now, it is important to note that you should not simply just choose the methodology that you like best, or that you feel more comfortable with. Yes, play to your strengths, but certainly don't go for qualitative methods just because you don't like stats. The methodology needs to be appropriate to your question.

6

Quantitative methodology

Research projects can be quantitative or qualitative, and it is important that you understand which method is the most appropriate and effective way of answering your research questions (identified in Chapter 5). This chapter will provide an overview of quantitative research methods, including a discussion of quantitative design, variable types and sampling techniques. We will also discuss how to write up your quantitative methodology chapter.

Learning outcomes

By the end of this chapter you will:

- Understand how research methodology maps on to your research question
- Be familiar with scientific methods relevant to quantitative research
- Understand elements of quantitative research design
- Understand sampling techniques relevant to quantitative research
- Understand how to write up your quantitative research methodology in your dissertation.

6.1 What is quantitative research, and when should you use it?

Quantitative research is generally described as research that involves the collection of numerical data, which is analysed using mathematical calculations (i.e. statistical analysis). It relies upon quantifiable constructs and measurements, the use of hypotheses and the inclusion of multiple variables, and is centred on determining the statistical significance of a relationship, or the difference between variables or groups. Quantitative research is generally large-scale, requiring a substantial sample size to achieve statistical power.

Quantitative methodology is rooted in scientific methods of investigation, where observations of organisms, activities and processes of the physical and social world are utilised to formulate knowledge and understanding. Quantitative research values such scientific methods alongside deductive logic, objectivity and the need to formulate and test hypotheses. This is a common epistemological approach in the social sciences, where the development of theory and knowledge is characterised by a continuous cycle of hypothesis formation, hypothesis testing and generation of new research questions. As such, existing research findings continuously influence the development of new research, building, over time, a greater knowledge and understanding of the field under investigation.

Put simply, quantitative methodology is appropriate when the research project involves testing a hypothesis about quantifiable variables. It is suitable for projects where you want to find out the nature of a relationship or difference between variables or groups, when you want to investigate cause and effect, or when you simply want to establish statistical evidence. Typically, quantitative research will involve the use of experimental design.

6.2 Experimental design

Experiments allow the researcher to investigate causality by manipulating one variable (the independent variable) to see if there is an effect on another variable (the dependent variable).

Independent variable: The variable you are manipulating (the thing you change between conditions)

Dependent variable: The variable you are measuring.

The independent variable(s) in a study can be manipulated in a variety of ways depending on the research question under investigation. For example, if you were interested in the effects of caffeine on attention, the independent variable 'caffeine' could be manipulated by giving participants either a caffeinated or decaffeinated drink prior to completing an attention task. In this example, attention would be the dependent variable (what you are measuring).

6.2.1 Between groups/independent measures designs

Using the above example, you might want your participants to complete just one condition of the experiment (i.e. either the caffeinated or decaffeinated condition). As such, your study would compare two *different* groups of participants (participants in the caffeinated group and participants in the decaffeinated group). This is known as a 'between groups' or 'independent measures' design.

Independent measures designs are used when you want to compare two *different* groups of participants. This might be particularly useful if you are interested in comparing groups that are naturally distinguishable from one another (e.g. males and females), but you can also apply an independent measures design to a study where the independent variable needs to be manipulated. In the example above, you can manipulate the drink that participants receive, such that one group will receive a caffeinated drink whilst the other group will receive a decaffeinated drink. There are various benefits to this type of design, listed below.

Benefits of independent measures designs

- They allow for comparison between two different groups.
- Participants only have to commit to one session: There is no repetition as participants are only taking part in one condition.
- Knowledge transfer or practice effects are not an issue: Participants only take part in one condition, so we do not need to worry about the effect that knowledge of one condition might have on their performance in another condition.
- Order effects do not need to be controlled for: If participants were taking part in multiple conditions (like in a repeated measures design, discussed below), we would need to control for order effects by randomising the order in which they complete the conditions, so that their experience of condition A does not affect their performance in condition B. With a simple two-condition study, this is fairly simple to do (50% of participants would do condition A first, followed by B, whilst the other 50% of participants would do condition B first, followed by A). However, the more conditions you have, and the more variables you have, the more complex this process becomes. Thankfully, with an independent measures design, we don't need to worry about this because participants will only be taking part in one condition.

Independent measures designs also have limitations. Firstly, this design may not be cost-effective. You need to recruit more participants – twice as many as you would need in a repeated measures design (discussed below), as you will have two *separate* groups of participants that you are trying to compare. As you need to ensure a sufficient sample size to achieve power in your analysis (discussed later), this can put a strain on recruitment and data collection procedures, which can take a long time.

It may also be difficult to ensure that your groups are comparable, because you cannot control for individual differences between participants that might affect the data. What we mean by this is that each participant will have their own individual circumstances, past experiences and characteristics, which could inadvertently have an impact on their individual data. For example, a participant who is experiencing life stressors may not be able to attend as well to the attention task as a participant who is not experiencing life stressors. Similarly, a participant who is suffering from a lack of sleep or illness may not perform as well as a participant who is in good health. In studies where participants take part in all conditions (repeated measures designs, discussed below), we would expect that a participant's individual circumstances and characteristics would have the same effect on all conditions they take part in. However, as participants in independent measures designs only take part in one condition, their individual differences could have an effect on the data obtained from that condition, affecting the validity of the findings.

Individual differences: Individual circumstances and characteristics that could have an effect on the data obtained from a participant.

6.2.2 Within groups/repeated measures designs

In an alternative design, you might ask participants to come back on two separate occasions so that they can complete *both* conditions in the experiment. Using the same caffeine and attention example as above, on one occasion your participants would be given the caffeinated drink, and on another occasion the same participants would return and would be given the decaffeinated drink, each followed by the completion of the attention task. This is known as a 'within groups' or 'repeated measures' design.

In the repeated measures example above, there are a number of confounds that we need to consider. Firstly, when conducting a repeated measures design, you would ideally need to control as much of the research setting as possible to prevent any confounding variables having an effect on the results. If you ask your participants to return on a separate occasion, you have very little control over their life in between conditions. As this experiment is looking at the effects of caffeine, you would need to ensure that your participants do not consume any caffeine prior to taking part in either experimental condition. This is a concern of the topic of study in general, but more so in a repeated measures design where you need to ensure that participants comply with the conditions of the study in the same way on two separate occasions. In addition, if you were conducting a repeated measures study, you'd also need to make sure that participants are in the same state on both occasions. Taking into account that there could be many other confounding variables affecting the participants' state of mind and attention span (e.g. sleep, stress, food), a repeated measures design is perhaps not best suited to this type of research question.

Secondly, we must also consider the possible effect on the results of asking participants to complete the same task twice – in this example, we are asking participants to complete the same attention task on two separate occasions. Unless there are significant differences between the items presented on the attention task in the two conditions (which throws up further issues with compatibility), it is likely that the participant will have familiarised themselves with the requirements and nature of the task by the time they complete it a second time. As a result, we might observe practice effects in the data, whereby participants might perform better on the second occasion, regardless of which condition they do first. In a similar vein, we might also observe order effects – where participants perform better in one condition as a result of experiencing the other condition first. For example, if all your participants took part in the decaffeinated condition first, followed by the caffeinated condition, it would be difficult to determine whether any increase in performance on the attention task the second time round was due to the caffeine they had consumed in the second condition, or whether it was simply due to practice effects. To overcome order effects, one technique is to counterbalance conditions, such that half your participants take part in the caffeinated condition first followed by the decaffeinated condition, and the other half of your participants take part in the decaffeinated condition first followed by the caffeinated condition. However, as already discussed, this may still give rise to practice effects when it comes to the attention task. So, as we have already established, a repeated measures design is perhaps not best suited to this type of research question.

Confounding variables: Variables that are not controlled for in your experiment but which may have an effect on the outcome of your study. These are sometimes also known as extraneous variables

Practice effects: An effect observed when participants are asked to complete the same task on multiple occasions, whereby performance improves over time, regardless of condition

Order effects: An effect that occurs due to the order in which participants complete tasks or conditions

Counterbalancing: Where half of your participants complete condition A first, followed by condition B, and the other half of your participants complete condition B first, followed by condition A.

Repeated measures studies can, however, be very effective when the researcher is interested in finding out how participants respond to multiple stimuli or situations. A classic example of a repeated measures study is the Stroop test (Stroop, 1935), where participants are asked to complete both conditions, and performance on the two conditions is then compared. Repeated measures designs can also be effective for investigating how participants' performance or responses change over time. For example, a study could ask the same participants to complete an attitude scale at multiple time points to see if and how their attitudes change over time. Similar studies can assess participants on an aptitude test at multiple time points to see how performance improves over time. This type of research is known as **longitudinal research.**

Benefits of repeated measures designs

- They are cost-effective: You need a smaller number of participants as you don't need to separate participants into experimental conditions because the same groups are being exposed to all treatments.
- We remove the confound of individual differences because the same subjects are used in all conditions. Any effect that individual differences have on one condition are therefore the same for all conditions.
- They allow the effect of treatment to be measured over time, and at multiple different times, using the same subjects.

Between groups/independent measures design: Where *different* participants take part in *each* condition of the independent variable

Within groups/repeated measures design: When the *same* participants take part in *all* conditions of the independent variable.

6.2.3 Matched pairs designs

One way of combatting the limitations of a repeated measures design is to conduct a matched pairs design. This is effectively an independent measures design where participants are put into pairs across groups, based on certain characteristics that could affect the data. This would be helpful if there was an obvious individual difference that could affect the outcome of the study. For example, going back to the caffeine and attention example, if there was evidence that gender or age had an effect on attention, each participant in the caffeinated group could be matched with a participant in the decaffeinated group on their gender and age. Matching participants in this way helps to overcome some of the individual differences that could affect the results in an independent measures design, whilst also avoiding the limitations of repeated measures designs. In this particular example, though, we should be mindful that there are plenty of other confounds that could play a role in the data, such as those mentioned above in the discussion of independent measures designs, and it would be near impossible to target all of these individual differences with a matched pairs design.

6.2.4 Mixed measures designs

Above, we have discussed the characteristics, benefits and limitations of independent and repeated measures designs. Whilst these methods are often employed individually, it is also common for research studies to employ elements of both independent and repeated measures designs within the same study. It is important to understand that *each* independent variable that you have in your study can be measured either between groups or within groups. As such, if you have multiple independent variables in your study, you can have some between groups variables and some within groups variables. In relation to the caffeine and attention study discussed earlier, an example of this type of design might be, for example, if you want to compare male and female participants (using gender as a between groups variable) on their performance on an attention task both before and after (using time as a within groups variable) drinking a caffeinated beverage. This would allow you to investigate whether the attention of male or female participants was more affected by caffeine.

Mixed methods designs can also be effective when investigating the effect of particular treatments or interventions. For example, if you wanted to investigate the effectiveness of a reading intervention, a mixed methods design would allow you to test participants at the pre- and the post-test (i.e. before and after the intervention) on their reading ability (repeated measures). You could then compare the performance of participants in the experimental condition (who were in receipt of the intervention) to participants in a control condition (who were not in receipt of the intervention), to determine which group (between groups variable) made most improvement. This would allow you to determine whether the intervention had been effective for improving reading ability in comparison to a control group.

6.3 Randomisation

One thing that is particularly important when planning your quantitative research project is the prospect of randomisation. This is applicable to both independent and repeated measures designs. Above, we have considered how randomisation can counteract the possible order effects that you might encounter when conducting repeated measures designs. However, randomisation is also important in independent measures designs where you need to consider how you will allocate participants to different groups. In some instances, such as when participants are already in predefined groups based on their natural characteristics (e.g. gender or age group), random allocation to groups is not applicable, but in most circumstances, you will need to ensure that participant assignment to experimental groups does not affect the results of the study. Let us explain how allocation to groups might be problematic. Say, for example, that you need a sample of 100 participants (50 in each group), and you allocate the first 50 people to sign up for your study to condition A (let's use the same example as earlier and say that condition A is the caffeine group), and the next 50 participants to condition B (the decaffeinated group). You might find that the group that received the caffeinated drink performed better on the attention task than the group receiving the decaffeinated drink. However, you couldn't be sure whether this finding is due to the caffeine, or due to the fact that the first 50 people to sign up to the study (the 50 people in this group) were simply keener to take part and therefore more engaged with the task. Random allocation can be used to overcome some of this potential bias. In repeated measures studies, random allocation can be used in a similar way to allocate participants to a starting condition when counterbalancing.

6.4 Research environment

6.4.1 Laboratory versus field experiments

The majority of face-to-face psychological research experiments will be conducted in a laboratory setting of some description, as this allows the researcher to have more control over the research environment and to eliminate confounding variables. However, by nature, laboratory studies are artificial, which reduces the ecological validity of the findings.

Alternatively, research can be carried out in a more naturalistic setting, where ecological validity is higher. However, this may compromise some elements of control, as there are many confounding variables in natural settings which could inadvertently affect the data, reducing the validity of the findings. Field experiments are popular in social psychological research, which is concerned with the impact of the environment, whereas lab experiments tend to be more popular in biological or cognitive psychology. Some benefits of laboratory and field experiments are highlighted in Table 6.1.

Table 6.1 Benefits of laboratory versus field experiments

Laboratory experiments	Field experiments
• More control over the research setting • Allow for manipulation of the independent variable • Possible to eliminate many confounding variables • Allow for replication of conditions • Allow for inclusion of a control group • Generally high reliability	• Take place in a natural setting – greater ecological and external validity • Allow for observations of people in different natural environments and situations • Better representativeness • Potential for larger scale research • Practical – can collect data in a natural setting without requiring participants to come into the lab • Relatively cost effective

6.4.2 Ensuring replicability

An important tenet of scientific methodology is the replicability of the study's findings. Refer to Chapter 3 and what we discussed about replications – findings need to be replicable in order to ensure validity. To some extent, the validity and reliability of findings from quantitative research are safeguarded by the quantitative nature of data, where numerical scales are used for measurement. For example, the numerical representation of human intelligence is the IQ score that can be measured using an intelligence test. The IQ score, as a quantified unit of measurement of human intelligence, enables researchers to maintain the same understanding over different levels of intelligence. The intelligence test, as a measurement of intelligence, therefore empowers the objective and replicable measurement of intelligence. The use of standardised assessments in quantitative research acts in a similar way, by utilising standard procedures for the administration of tests, and the measurement and scoring of data. However, in many instances, other controls on the research environment need to be put in place in order to secure the replicability of the research. To address this, quantitative studies often involve the use of controlled settings.

6.4.2.1 Controlled settings

Laboratory settings can be controlled in a number of ways. For example, we can control the physical properties of the environment such as the lighting, temperature and sounds. We can also control the conditions that participants are exposed to, more so than we would be able to in a more natural setting. For example, sleep researchers can subject participants to sleep deprivation in a sleep lab by controlling the amount of sleep that participants are allowed to have during a given time frame. This manipulation allows sleep researchers to investigate the effects of sleep deprivation on their participants' cognitive abilities, whilst also controlling other confounding variables (e.g. by ensuring that they all consume the same foods). This can be beneficial for this type of research, but it is highly unlikely that you would be conducting this type of research for your dissertation. The type of controlled settings that you're more likely to use in your dissertation research include things like controlling the time participants have or the music that participants listen to whilst completing a particular task.

Controlled settings

Controlled settings allow researchers to limit the influence of confounding variables over participants' responses or performance.

It is important that you report as much detail as possible about your research setting in your methodology chapter, so that conditions can be replicated in future, to test the validity of your findings.

6.5 Non-experimental quantitative research methodology

6.5.1 Correlational studies

Correlational studies are maybe the most widely used non-experimental quantitative methodology used in undergraduate dissertation projects. Correlational design is a type of observation that gathers information about two or more variables in conditions where a properly controlled experiment is not possible, or the research question is more about observing the relationship between variables than the differences. Correlational studies are widely used in quantitative research in psychology but are most prominent in social, health and clinical psychology.

Correlations allow us to determine whether a relationship exists between two variables, how strong this relationship is and importantly the direction of this relationship. For example, if you are interested in the relationship between hours of sleep and exam grades, a correlational design would allow you to determine (a) whether there is a relationship between the amount of sleep someone has and how well they perform in an exam, and (b) whether there is a positive or negative relationship between these two variables. A positive correlation is one where both variables increase at a similar rate (in this example, as sleep increases, exam grades also increase); a negative correlation is one where as one variable increases, the other decreases (in this example, as sleep increases, exam grades decrease). In this example, it would make sense to expect that there would be a positive correlation between sleep and exam performance.

However, whilst a correlational design is suitable if your research question is dealing with relationships between variables, it is important to note that correlation does not imply causality. As such, you will not be able to observe cause and effect from a simple correlation analysis.

6.5.2 Cross-sectional and longitudinal studies

Cross-sectional and longitudinal studies are probably the quantitative research methodology designs that you are least likely to use in an undergraduate project, mainly because they are both complex and time-consuming, which is often beyond the remit of a dissertation module. Nevertheless, it is always useful to remind yourself of some research methodology terminology that you might come across when you are designing your dissertation research project.

Cross-sectional studies are a type of observational study, like correlational, with the main difference being that cross-sectional studies are based on observations that we make *between different groups or populations* at a single point in time. This type of research methodology is common in developmental, clinical and health psychology. An example of a cross-sectional design would be observing the levels of motivation between male and female final-year students. Note that the gender groups are naturally defined here, so you are not manipulating any variables, but you are still measuring different groups. Whilst it would be correct to describe this as a between groups design, it would be more accurate to describe the design as cross-sectional.

A longitudinal study can be very similar to a cross-sectional study, with the difference being that observations are made *over a period of time*. Longitudinal research is popular in developmental psychology – for example, looking at children's reading development over time, or looking at how older people's cognitive skills differ as they age.

6.6 Participants in quantitative research: Sample size, recruitment and ethics

It is highly likely that as psychologists, your participants will be people. The sample sizes in different types of study will vary significantly, but quantitative research by its nature will usually require a far larger sample of participants than qualitative research. But how do you know what sample size is appropriate for your methodology?

6.6.1 Calculating the appropriate sample size for your project

There are two main ways in which you can justify your decision over the sample size for your project. The simplest way is to refer to previous research in the area – what sample sizes have been used in existing research? Referring to studies with a similar methodology to your own design should give an indication of the approximate sample size that would be appropriate for your own study, and at undergraduate level, this should be sufficient to justify your sample size. However, for top marks, you need to consider how you will achieve power in your analysis in order to ensure that your results are reliable. To impress your examiners, we would recommend you consider calculating your sample size by running a power analysis, such as G*power, which allows you to calculate statistical power for a wide variety of statistical analyses including t-tests, ANOVA and chi-square tests. Of course, in order to run this power analysis, you will need first to know what type of analysis you plan to use – so perhaps a little more planning will be required. Remember what we discussed earlier though, that your data analysis strategy will map on from your methodology, and importantly, from your research question – so, essentially, once you have decided on your research question and design, your method of data analysis should be dictated by the decisions that have already been made. In order to run your power analysis using G*power, you must also be able to identify the number of variables, the number of conditions of your variables, *and* either the desired effect size, desired significance level or the desired power. You can find out more about all of these elements in your specialist research methods textbooks and can locate a freely available G*power calculator online.

6.6.2 Recruitment methods

There are many ways you can recruit participants for your research project. The methods for recruiting participants are known as sampling techniques. Many sampling techniques can be used for quantitative or qualitative research, so you will see some overlap between this section and the material in Chapter 7.

Sampling techniques

Sampling techniques are the methods you use to recruit a sample of participants for your study from a population. The **target population** is the total number of potential participants from which a sample will be recruited. In order to ensure that the findings are generalisable to the wider population, you will need to ensure that your sample is representative.

- **Random sampling**: where participants are selected at random from the target population. Every member of the target population has an equal chance of being selected. Random sampling provides the best chance of gaining a representative sample, particularly when working with large populations. However, this can be very time-consuming, and is not suitable for many types of study, particularly where the researcher might not have full access to all members of the specified population.
- **Stratified sampling**: where the target population is split into subcategories, and the researcher makes a conscious effort to ensure that the split of participants in the sample is representative of the split of members in the target population. For example, if one in four members of the general population have blue eyes, one in four participants in the sample must also have blue eyes (if eye colour is relevant to the topic under investigation). Whilst this method helps to ensure that the sample is representative of the population, it can be very time-consuming, as appropriate subcategories have to be identified and proportions need to be calculated before participants can be recruited.
- **Systematic sampling**: where participants are selected in an orderly fashion from the target population. Sample selection is based on each member's position within a list of those in the target population, and the positions selected are based on the target sample size in comparison to the size of the population. For example, if you want to recruit 100 participants from a population of 500, you would select every fifth person on the list. Whilst this technique generally results in a fairly representative sample, it can be difficult to employ as you would need a list of all members of the population to begin with.
- **Opportunity sampling**: where the researcher selects participants who are available at the time. This is a recruitment method based on convenience and can also be called convenience sampling. This is perhaps the most common sampling technique in psychological research, particularly at undergraduate level, as it is efficient and economical. However, it is likely to form samples that are unrepresentative of the population and which can be heavily biased by the researcher.
- **Purposive sampling**: where the researcher starts with a purpose in mind, and purposefully targets a specific type of participant, excluding any participants who don't fit the intended characteristics. This can be beneficial if the researcher wants to recruit participants with specific characteristics but is likely to yield a biased and unrepresentative sample.
- **Volunteer sampling**: where participants are volunteers who have actively chosen to take part in the study. This is also known as a self-selecting sample. Adverts are often used, and participants volunteer by responding to the advert. This is fairly convenient, and is the most ethical form of sampling, as participants are required to personally sign up rather than being approached by the researcher. However, it is likely to form an unrepresentative sample, biased by the characteristics of participants who are likely to respond to an advertisement.

(Continued)

- **Snowball sampling**: where participants are asked to recommend other potential participants to take part in the study. This creates a 'snowball effect' whereby the researcher recruits one participant and asks them to refer the study to another participant, and then they refer the study to a third participant, and so on. This can be particularly useful when the researcher has limited access to the specified population. This is also known as referral sampling or chain sampling.

6.7 Materials/measures

At this stage, you should have decided what type of quantitative research methodology is more appropriate for your research design and what your variables will be. Now you need to think about the materials that you will use in your study and how you are going to measure your variables. It is imperative to use materials and measures that are relevant to your research design and research questions. A common mistake that undergraduate students make when thinking about their materials is proposing the use of measures of variables that are not relevant to their research question. For example, a questionnaire on participants' cultural background should only be administrated if cultural background is a variable in the design of your study.

The most common way in which we measure variables in psychology is through the use of questionnaires (standardised or not standardised), observations (sometimes using specialised equipment such as fMRI or an eye tracker) or standardised assessments (e.g. of participants' cognitive abilities). In order to identify the most appropriate measure(s) for the variables in your study, you will need to consider the existing research literature carefully, and also discuss the options with your supervisor to determine what equipment and resources are available to you within your department.

6.7.1 Questionnaires

Amongst the most popular types of measures used by undergraduate students are questionnaires. Questionnaires can be a useful measure of a multitude of factors and can be administered in either face-to-face studies or online studies, making them flexible for different methods of data collection.

If you are thinking of using a questionnaire in your study, consider whether there is a standardised measure available to you that is already in existence that might be suitable for use within your study (e.g. a questionnaire on anxiety levels). In many cases, however, it is likely that an existing questionnaire may need to be adapted or modified in some way to meet the aim(s) and research question(s) of your study. As long as you have ethical approval to use a modified version of such a scale, and if you have justified your reasons for needing to modify it, this is perfectly acceptable. In other cases, you might want to consider creating a questionnaire specifically for the purpose of your research project.

6.8 Writing your quantitative methodology chapter

The methodology chapter of any research report, whether at undergraduate level, postgraduate level or as a professional researcher, and whether the research is quantitative or qualitative, should always contain the four main sub-sections: design, participants, materials and procedure. You should also report on the main ethical considerations for your project – this can be in a stand-alone subsection or written as part of the procedure. Here, we have provided a brief guide of what details to include in each of these subsections. It's important to note that the methodology chapter should be written in the past tense in your research report as, by the time we read it, it will have already been done!

6.8.1 Design

In the design section of your methodology for a quantitative report, you need to clearly report the type of design you have employed and the independent variable(s) (and levels of your independent variables) involved in the study. You also need to identify your dependent variable and make it clear how your dependent variable was operationalised (i.e. how it was measured). For example, you might write something like, 'A 2 (gender: male or female) x 2 (condition: caffeinated or decaffeinated) mixed design was employed to investigate the effects of gender and caffeine on participants' performance on an attention task, where gender was a within groups variable and condition was a between groups variable.'

6.8.2 Participants

The participants subsection of the method is where you identify and explain information about your sample of participants. It is important that you are able to provide sufficient information to allow for replication of your study in the future, and that another researcher can recruit a comparable sample for such a replication. In this section, you therefore need to identify the following information:

- The number of participants who took part
- The number of males and females in your sample
- The age range and mean age of your sample

- The numbers of participants in each group (relevant to each independent variable)
- The sampling technique that was used to recruit your participants
- Details of where your participants were recruited from (without providing any personally identifying information)
- Any inclusion/exclusion criteria that were relevant during the recruitment process.

For example, you might write something like:

One hundred and eight participants were recruited via opportunity sampling from a university in the West Midlands area. The sample consisted of 58 females and 50 males aged between 18 and 26 years, with a mean age of 20 years and six months. All participants took part in both the caffeine and decaffeinated conditions, but the order of conditions was counterbalanced such that half of the participants completed the caffeinated condition first, followed by the decaffeinated condition, whilst the other half of the participants completed the decaffeinated condition first, followed by the caffeinated condition. Participants were randomly assigned to an order (identified as either order '1' (caffeinated followed by decaffeinated) or order '2' (decaffeinated followed by caffeinated)) using a random number generator. Participants who had any medical condition likely to be heightened by caffeine were excluded from the study.

6.8.3 Materials

In the materials subsection of the method, you need to explain the materials and measures you have used in your study in sufficient detail (again, to allow replication). For each measure that you have used, you need to explain the details of administration, what participants were required to do and how participants were scored (i.e. how the administration of each measure resulted in data for your study). For standardised assessments, some of these details will be reported in the user manuals, but it is important that you provide some level of explanation here too. You will also need to mention any details of software that was used, and any additional relevant technical information. You *do not* need to mention things like pens, paper or a computer here, nor do you need to refer to ethical forms such as the participant information sheet and consent form as materials for the study. The fact that you presented participants with these ethical forms can be mentioned in the procedure, but they are not strictly classed as research materials, so you can omit to mention them in the materials subsection.

6.8.4 Procedure

The procedure is the last of the four main sections that you will need to report in your methodology chapter. The procedure should report, in chronological order, everything that your participants were subjected to as part of their participation in the study. For example, you will need to mention that participants were firstly presented with a participant information sheet and asked to sign an informed consent form before taking part in the study. You'll then need to explain what happened during the course of the study, step by step – in as much detail as possible to allow for replication.

6.9 Strengths and challenges of quantitative research

Some of the strengths and challenges of quantitative research are outlined in Table 6.2.

Table 6.2   Strengths and challenges of quantitative research

Strengths	Challenges
• Allows us to test larger samples than qualitative research, meaning findings are likely to be more representative of the wider population • Allows us to test for significance • Allows us to test hypotheses • Allows us to test for differences between groups, relationships between variables, and effects • Longitudinal research can provide evidence of how participants' abilities, opinions, etc. change over time • Standardised assessments provide a reliable measure of participants' abilities • There is usually a clear theoretical framework • Provides a statistical, scientific answer to a question • Can be conducted in a natural setting or in a lab • Methods such as surveys can be very cost-effective • Data are fairly quick to analyse • Multiple types of data can be collected within a single study, and multiple analyses can be conducted	• It is often difficult to recruit sufficient sample sizes, especially if inclusion criteria are limiting • It can sometimes be difficult to control variables and confounds • May require specialist equipment, software and tools • Data collection can be a lengthy process • Problems can arise with data not meeting parametric assumptions; transforming data can be laborious • Can easily become overcomplicated • Does not capture details of the participants' experiences, emotions, attitudes or values, etc.

Homework

Use the guidance in this chapter to help you begin to draft the structure of your methodology chapter. For every decision you make, ensure that you are able to justify why you have chosen to design your study in this way.

Chapter summary

In this chapter, we have considered a range of quantitative research methods, including a discussion of quantitative design, variable types and sampling techniques. It is important that you consider and are able to justify each of these decisions when planning your study.

We have also discussed how to write up your quantitative methodology chapter.

Checklist

✓ Decide on the most appropriate design to help you answer your research question.

✓ Decide on the variables for your study and how you will measure them.

✓ Make a start on writing your methodology chapter.

7

Qualitative methodology

As explored in Chapter 6, it is important that you understand which method is the most appropriate and effective way of answering your research questions. Qualitative methodology is very different from quantitative and allows a deeper exploration of your participants' experiences or viewpoints. In this chapter, we will explore qualitative research design. The chapter will guide you through the development of interview schedules, discuss different interview techniques and provide guidance for working with participants in qualitative research settings.

Learning outcomes

By the end of this chapter you will:

- Understand the key elements of qualitative research design
- Understand different methods of collecting qualitative data
- Understand how to develop interview schedules
- Understand methods of working with participants in qualitative research, including ethical considerations
- Understand how to write up your qualitative research methodology.

7.1 What is qualitative research and when should you use it?

Qualitative research is the in-depth study of personal experiences, attitudes and values, usually through the use of interviews or focus groups. Qualitative research involves the collection of data looking at participants' written or spoken (articulated) responses. The sample size in qualitative research is usually quite small, to allow for an in-depth exploration of individual participants' experiences and attitudes.

Qualitative research is suitable if you want to find out how participants feel about something, or what their opinions or attitudes are towards a particular phenomenon. Qualitative research is also often used when you want to gain a deep and meaningful insight into participants' lived experiences. By its nature, qualitative research allows you to analyse participants' detailed accounts of situations, attitudes and values, meaning that it provides you with rich and meaningful data about the topic under investigation. This is in comparison to quantitative research, which focuses more on quantifying outputs to provide evidence of statistical significance (see Chapter 6).

7.2 Qualitative research design

As we have already established, qualitative research is concerned with the collection of detailed, rich data from participants. This can be obtained in a number of different ways, namely through the use of interviews, focus groups or surveys. We will discuss each of these methods in turn below. Make sure you read each section carefully when considering which methodology might be most suitable for helping you to answer your research question(s).

7.2.1 Interviews

Interviews are perhaps the most commonly used method of data collection in qualitative research. There are three main types of interview that you should consider before deciding on a structure that is most suitable for your project: structured, unstructured and semi-structured interviews.

Structured interviews: Structured interviews are the most formal type of interview. Questions are asked in a set, predefined order, and there is very limited flexibility in the way the questions can be asked. These types of interviews are often common for job applicants, as they allow for consistency and fairness across interviewees. Structured interviews are also fairly quick, as questions are typically closed-ended, meaning that responses are likely to be much shorter than in less structured interviews. However, this can mean that responses are limited and lack detail – meaning you're unlikely to get the rich and meaningful data you might want in a qualitative research study.

Unstructured interviews: Unstructured interviews are the least structured and least formal type of interview. They are typically made up of a few open-ended questions, allowing participants to respond freely and in depth, without any interference from the researcher. These open-ended questions can be asked in any order, with great flexibility – questions can be added, changed or removed throughout the interview, depending on the participant's responses.

Whilst this allows the participant to shape the discussion, the unstructured nature of this type of interview also allows the researcher to ask additional questions to probe for more information. The process of conducting an unstructured interview can, however, be very time-consuming, as there is no control over how long the interview will last.

Semi-structured interviews: Semi-structured interviews offer the researcher the best of both worlds. Typically consisting of a detailed interview schedule, the questions in a semi-structured interview are flexible in terms of the order in which they are asked. These characteristics of a semi-structured interview provide the researcher with an opportunity to direct the discussion appropriately towards the intended topics, but also allow the flexibility to shape the discussion in a way that aids the natural flow of conversation with the participant. For this reason, semi-structured interviews are usually the most popular type of interview used in psychological research. Some strengths and limitations for each type of interview are listed in Table 7.1.

Table 7.1   Strengths and limitations of each type of interview schedule

Interview type	Strengths	Limitations
Structured	<ul><li>Formal</li><li>Allows the researcher to restrict and control the conversation</li><li>The participant cannot go off at a tangent in the discussion</li><li>Fairly quick to conduct</li><li>Easy to replicate</li><li>Allows fairness between participants as everyone is asked the same questions in the same order</li><li>Useful in job interviews</li></ul>	<ul><li>No flexibility – the questions and order in which they are asked are both rigid</li><li>Less opportunity for the researcher to build rapport with the participant</li><li>The participant has no opportunity to steer the conversation in a particular direction, meaning that data can be limited in explaining participants' true experiences/feelings</li><li>Often involves closed questions which generate short responses</li></ul>
Semi-structured	<ul><li>Gives the researcher flexibility in using an interview schedule, changing the order and/or wording of questions depending on participants' responses</li><li>Allows the participant to speak freely about their experiences whilst also allowing the researcher to control the direction of the conversation</li><li>Allows for a combination of closed- and open-ended questions</li></ul>	<ul><li>Does not allow complete control over the interview</li></ul>

(Continued)

Table 7.1   (Continued)

Interview type	Strengths	Limitations
Unstructured	<ul><li>Informal</li><li>Gives the researcher flexibility to use a loose interview schedule, or not use one at all</li><li>Open-ended questions allow the participant to steer the discussion and speak freely</li><li>Questions can be adapted, changed or omitted depending on the participant's response to each question</li><li>Allows the researcher to prompt and probe the participant for further information or explanation</li></ul>	<ul><li>The researcher has little control over the discussion and little opportunity to steer the conversation</li><li>Can be very time-consuming as there is no certainty over how long each interview will last</li><li>Similarly, data analysis can be lengthier, due to the length of the interview but also due to flexibility from one participant to another</li><li>Requires the researcher to be able to build rapport with participants</li></ul>

7.2.2 Focus groups

Focus groups are essentially group interviews – a group of participants would be interviewed together, prompted by the researcher. Focus groups aim to encourage collaborative responses and build a strong group dynamic amongst focus group members, facilitating the interaction and discussion through the use of prompts and questions from the researcher. Rather than taking an active role in the discussion though, the researcher's role in a focus group is to ensure that the group of participants interact with one another, and to try to keep the discussion on track. Focus groups are usually structured to some extent by a set of interview questions, but, rather than forming an interview schedule, they are used to guide the discussion in a particular direction in order to obtain data on the desired topic(s).

Focus groups are useful when you want to observe the way in which participants interact with one another, or how they respond to discussion points in a group. They can provide a good opportunity to observe features of the interaction other than speech, such as humour, conflict or hostility between different group members.

Data from focus groups can also be more naturalistic, as focus groups provide an opportunity to obtain information that is divulged in a more natural conversation (than a one-to-one interview) between participants who have likely experienced similar circumstances or expressed similar attitudes. This is in comparison to a one-to-one interview where the participant might feel as though they are being judged by the interviewer, no matter how hard the interviewer might try to appear warm and welcoming. However, in some cases, participants may be reluctant to divulge personal experiences or sensitive information in a focus group, whereas they may be more likely to talk about these topics on a one-to-one basis. As such, you should consider whether a focus group is likely to be effective for yielding useful, accurate and meaningful data from your participants.

It is also important to consider the research methodology from a practical perspective. Focus groups can be very difficult to conduct if you have not been trained in the relevant skills. As a researcher, you need to be able to build rapport with your participants as a group, and need to be able to read the situation in order to know when it is appropriate to probe participants for more information or when to prompt them to steer the discussion in the right direction, without influencing participants' responses in any way. Some strengths and challenges of using focus groups are outlined in Table 7.2.

Table 7.2   Strengths and challenges of using focus groups

Strengths	Challenges
• Group interviews allow participants to discuss the topic under investigation between them in depth • Allows the researcher to observe interactions and conversations between participants within a group • Participants may feel more comfortable discussing a particular issue with other participants who are in a similar situation, in comparison to talking individually to a researcher	• Participants may feel shy or uncomfortable discussing their experiences in a group • Can be difficult to identify individual participants in the recording, and likewise to ensure details remain confidential • Can be difficult to keep the conversation on track as group discussions are likely to go off at a tangent • Can be subject to social desirability if participants feel the need to impress other group members • Relies on rapport amongst group members • Relies on a group of participants all being available to attend the study at one time, which can make recruitment difficult

7.3 Developing your materials

In considering quantitative research (Chapter 6), we discussed the process of identifying and using standardised assessments which will already have been developed for use in research to test standardised structures. In some instances, even quantitative researchers might find that the scales they locate are not completely suitable for studying the topic or research question in their project, and existing measures may therefore need to be amended accordingly. In qualitative research, this is more common, as your research question and aims are likely to be more specific and detailed. In most qualitative projects, therefore, you will need to develop your own measure(s), namely an interview schedule.

7.3.1 Interview schedules

As we have already established, the most common method of collecting qualitative data is through the use of one-to-one, usually face-to-face, interviews, or through the use of focus groups. But how do you know what to ask your participants? Below, we have provided a step-by-step guide to creating your interview schedule.

Step 1: Familiarise yourself with the literature

The questions included in your interview schedule should be rooted in psychological literature – there needs to be a reason *why* you are asking certain questions, and these questions should have a clear link to the aims of your research project.

Step 2: Identify relevant subtopics or areas of interest linked to your research aims

Familiarising yourself with the literature (in step 1) will help you to identify particular themes and subtopics that might be relevant to your research. These will lead to the identification of potential interview questions in step 3.

Step 3: Develop key topics into questions

Using the subtopics and evidence from existing literature, what might you need to ask participants about in order to obtain a full and detailed picture of their experiences or attitudes about the phenomenon under investigation? Start to use these subtopics to shape the development of potential questions for your interview schedule.

Step 4: Order questions logically to aid the flow of conversation

Once you have a basic list of questions that you want to ask participants, it is important to think about how the conversation will flow – you don't want to abruptly switch from topic to topic, so think about the order in which it would make most sense to cover the topics under investigation, and consider adding linking questions where relevant to improve the flow. Of course, if you are planning to conduct a semi- or unstructured interview, the order of questions is likely to change, but it is useful to have a guide to keep the conversation flowing.

Step 5: Consider adding prompts and probes for more information

Finally, you should consider *how* your participants might respond to each of the questions you ask. Put yourself in the shoes of your participant for a moment and imagine that you were asked each of the questions on your interview schedule. Are there any questions that might elicit a closed response? For example, questions that begin with 'Do you...?' or 'Did you...?' are known as 'closed questions', as they could lead to a very short (yes/no) response. You should also be careful of using leading questions – you want your participants to provide an honest and true account of their experiences or attitudes, and therefore you should avoid influencing them in any way. Instead, consider using questions that give participants a chance to respond openly, such as 'How did that make you feel?', or following a short answer probe for more information, such as 'Could you explain what you mean by that?' or 'Could you tell me a bit more about that?'.

Step 6: Practise and revise

If you haven't conducted qualitative research of your own before (which is likely to be the case for dissertation students), it would be advisable to consider testing out your interview schedule before you begin using it to collect data. As we discussed above, methods such as focus groups can be very difficult to conduct if you haven't been properly trained in how to respond to participants and how to read the discussion to know when to intervene. Similarly, with interviews you need to know when it is appropriate to ask for more information from your participant. As such, practising your interview with a friend or peer can be helpful in preparing you for data collection in a number of ways. Firstly, practice helps you to understand what to expect in the interview, and helps you prepare for working with your participants. Practice is also useful for identifying which types of questions elicit the responses you are looking for (i.e. detailed enough and on topic), where there might be any problems, and where prompts and probes might be useful. As a result, you might need to further amend your schedule to take account of these preliminary findings before you begin the data collection phase.

Examples of good interview questions

- Questions that are **direct, short** and **simple to understand**
- **Open-ended** questions – these provide your participants with an opportunity to talk freely about the topic.

Examples of bad interview questions

- Questions that are **too long**
- Questions that are **double-barrelled** – two questions in one

(Continued)

- **Leading questions** – questions that influence your participants' responses
- **Ambiguous** questions – questions that are unclear and difficult to understand
- Questions that use **complex language** or **jargon** – questions that use unnecessarily complex or specialist language
- **Closed questions** – questions that elicit short 'yes' or 'no' responses, providing limited data.

7.3.2 Developing a qualitative questionnaire

You can use many of the principles of interview design to help you to develop a qualitative questionnaire or survey, as survey questions need to adhere to similar standards. For example, they must be simple, direct and easy to understand and be free of complex language or jargon. This is particularly important in research utilising questionnaires as participants are unlikely to have an opportunity to ask questions to clarify your intentions and expectations, particularly if you are hoping to conduct your questionnaire online. We have already discussed the use of questionnaires in quantitative research, but it is important to recognise that surveys and questionnaires can also be used effectively to gather qualitative data. It is important to use open-ended questions in qualitative surveys to encourage participants to provide as much detail as possible in their answers – survey data has the potential to be significantly less detailed than spoken data, as there is no way of prompting participants for more information.

7.4 Working with participants in qualitative research

As with quantitative methods, there are various options when it comes to recruiting participants for qualitative research. Some of the most common sampling techniques are outlined in section 6.6.2 and overlap with qualitative methodologies.

7.4.1 Building rapport

In Chapter 2 we discussed the importance of building and managing a relationship with your supervisor. In qualitative research, it is just as important (if not more so) to build a relationship, or at least a rapport, with your participants. The way you respond to them will have an effect on how they respond to you, so it is important to be friendly and accepting, but to maintain the researcher–participant dynamic. This is important for a number of reasons. Firstly, consider the importance of your participants. You probably need them a lot more than they need you, so it is imperative that you are able to make them feel at ease, but also that professionally and subtly you maintain control of the way in which the interview is conducted. Secondly, consider the subject you are researching.

In qualitative research, it is common for researchers to be investigating complex and/or extremely sensitive topics, so you need to ensure that your participant feels comfortable in the research environment, but also that you do not feel intimidated or vulnerable as a researcher. In planning your project, you will therefore need to think about the ethical considerations relevant to protecting both your participants *and* yourself.

7.4.2 Ethics for working with participants in qualitative research settings

There are many more considerations than those discussed here, so the information provided in this section should be considered alongside Chapter 9 on general ethical considerations. In this section, we explain the main considerations that you should take into account when working with participants in *qualitative* research settings.

7.4.2.1 The principle of no harm

The most important ethical consideration is about protecting both yourself and your participants from any physical or psychological harm. It is necessary therefore to consider how to treat participants – how you will interact with them and obtain data from them. When you apply for ethical approval, it is important to consider how you will mitigate any potential risks. For example, if your research is investigating a particularly sensitive topic, such as abortion or terrorism, you need to consider the impact that this might have on your participants' psychological wellbeing. You may also need to identify appropriate sources of support for participants if they become distressed or uncomfortable during the research process – who/where will you refer them to? You will need to be aware of these sources of support in advance of working with any participants, so that you are prepared for any eventuality. Whilst we are discussing participants' feeling uncomfortable, we should consider their right to withdraw or not to answer potentially upsetting questions.

7.4.2.2 The right to refuse/withdraw

It is of utmost importance that your participants understand their right to refuse to answer any question that they feel uncomfortable with, and their right to withdraw from the study if they no longer wish to continue. This is particularly important in qualitative research where participants may easily become upset or uncomfortable as a result of the discussions that take place during their participation. If you experience a participant becoming distressed during the study, you should end the interview and direct them to sources of further support.

7.4.2.3 Anonymity

In a similar vein, it is reasonable for participants in any research to expect that their responses will be anonymous. In qualitative research, this is even more important as it is likely that participants will reveal highly private and sensitive information about their experiences, attitudes and values. Researchers have a duty to safeguard their participants both against any harm resulting from participation in the research, and from any external risk of harm that might become apparent during the research. For example, the researcher needs to make it clear that any concerns they have about the mental or physical wellbeing of the participant may need to be passed on to the relevant authorities or agencies. Qualitative researchers also have a duty to ensure that data remain completely anonymous in the write-up of the results, and that any identifiable information about the individual participant, their contacts or linking organisations is suitably redacted or anonymised (e.g. by using pseudonyms) throughout the report. Of course, in some cases, anonymity is complex. For example, you might be working with organisations or individuals who are not easily disguised by simply changing their names or redacting what you consider to be 'identifiable information'. Alternatively, your participants may *want* to be identified. In these cases, researchers can use a signed release form, confirming their agreement and authorising you to report identifiable characteristics about them in your written report. It is unlikely that you would come across this in your dissertation project, but it is something to be mindful of – discuss this with your supervisor/ethics board if you think it may be relevant to your project.

7.4.2.4 Confidentiality

Confidentiality is tricky in qualitative research. Whilst it is a reasonable expectation of research participation that the information you reveal will be treated confidentially, qualitative research comes with the understanding that the content of an interview or focus group will be transcribed and analysed as part of the research. We must also consider the principle of no harm (as discussed above): as a researcher, you have the responsibility to ensure the safety of your participants, so even when data *can* be kept completely confidential, you might sometimes need to break this promise in order to protect your participant(s) or other people. This might be apparent if you are working with children or vulnerable adults and have concerns about their safety or wellbeing.

Practical advice for qualitative research

- Ensure that you have a good quality digital voice recorder to record your interviews, and test this out in advance.

- Conduct your interviews in a quiet space to avoid interference from background noise in the recording.
- Take spare batteries for your voice recorder!

7.5 Writing your qualitative methodology chapter

As with a quantitative research methodology chapter, your methodology for a qualitative report should contain four main subsections: design, participants, materials and procedure. Here, we provide some guidance about what to include in each section.

7.5.1 Design

You should begin your design section by identifying that you have taken a qualitative approach in designing your study, and by describing how you have addressed your research question (e.g. have you employed an inter-view, focus group or survey?) You also need to identify the topic under investigation and justify why the chosen design is appropriate for this particular study. You might write something like, 'A qualitative design was employed in which semi-structured interviews were used to investigate participants' lived experiences of social anxiety in higher education. Semi-structured interviews were identified as being most appropriate as they allow for flexibility whilst also allowing the researcher to structure the discussion to focus on relevant subtopics.'

7.5.2 Participants

As in a report on quantitative methodology, your qualitative methodology chapter should contain descriptive information about your sample of participants. It is important that you provide sufficient information about your sample to allow for replication of your study in future, and so that another researcher can recruit a comparable sample for such a replication. You can find a list of information that you need to report in the participants section, in section 6.8.2 of this book. For example, you might write something like, 'Eight participants were recruited via opportunity sampling from a university in the West Midlands area. The sample consisted of four females and two males, aged between 18 and 23 years, with a mean age of 19 years and 2 months. All participants took part in the semi-structured interviews individually, on university campus, between the hours of 9am and 5pm. Inclusion criteria specified that participants must be students in higher education, and that they must have experienced social anxiety during this period of study. Any participants with severe mental health issues were excluded from the study to avoid heightening their symptoms.'

7.5.3 Materials

The materials section of the methodology is where you explain the development of your qualitative materials. For example, if you have developed an interview schedule for use in your study, this section of the methodology is where you will explain not only how this schedule was used in the study, but also how the schedule was designed in the first place. It is important to justify the inclusion of certain questions and topics, with reference to existing research literature where relevant. For example, you might write something like, 'A semi-structured interview schedule was developed for use in this study, consisting of 16 questions. Existing research has identified that having supportive friendships is an important factor in coping with social anxiety at university (Reference, 20XX), so the interview included questions such as "Do you feel that your friends are supportive of your social anxiety?" followed by "Could you explain to me how your friends help you manage your social anxiety?". The interview was designed to last approximately 20 minutes and included the use of prompts and probes which could be used to gain further information from participants when necessary.'

7.5.4 Procedure

As with quantitative methodology, the procedure is the last of the four main sections of your qualitative methodology chapter. The procedure should report, in chronological order, everything involved in being a participant in the study. This should include details of ethics, such as presenting participants with a participant information sheet and asking them to sign an informed consent form, followed by details of the study. It is particularly important to explain that participants were debriefed (explaining how) when you are researching sensitive topics such as those that might be explored through qualitative research. Remember to write concisely, providing sufficient information to allow for replication.

7.6 Strengths and challenges of qualitative research

Some of the strengths and challenges of qualitative research are listed in Table 7.3.

Table 7.3   Strengths and challenges of qualitative research

Strengths	Challenges
• Less need to control for conditions or be concerned about statistical power • More flexible • Allows deeper exploration of participants' lived experiences, attitudes and values • Rarely requires specialist equipment • Interview schedules can be designed around your topic area, rather than seeking standardised assessments • Allows for participants to lead the course of conversation (with structured and semi-structured interviews) • Interviews and focus groups can usually be conducted in a range of settings, meaning participants don't necessarily need to come into a lab • Data collection is fairly quick	• Usually only allows collection of one type of data • Much smaller sample sizes than quantitative research, meaning it is more difficult to argue the generalisability of findings • Can sometimes be difficult to access specific populations, especially if the research is on a sensitive topic • Theoretical framework is less certain • Cannot establish cause and effect or statistical evidence • Transcription is a lengthy process, taking an average of one hour per ten minutes of recording • Data analysis can be time-consuming, as you will need to read and revisit the data a number of times

Chapter summary

In this chapter, we have considered qualitative research design. We have discussed the development of interview schedules and different interview techniques, and provided guidance for working with participants in qualitative research settings.

It is important to recognise the differences between quantitative and qualitative research design, and the benefits and challenges of each type of research, and to be able to identify the most appropriate methodology for your study. The information provided in this chapter should help you to define the specifics of your qualitative research design.

Homework

Use the guidance in this chapter to help you to begin to draft the structure of your methodology chapter. For every decision you make, ensure that you are able to justify why you have chosen to design your study in this way.

Checklist

✓ Identify the most appropriate method for addressing your research question.

✓ Locate or develop your research materials. This may be an interview schedule – you can use the information presented in this chapter to help you to create your questions.

✓ Make sure that you can justify the decisions you have made throughout the process of designing your study.

✓ Start to write up your methodology chapter.

8

Mixed Methods Research Projects

So far, we have explored quantitative and qualitative methodologies separately in Chapters 6 and 7. The majority of undergraduate dissertations will be either quantitative *or* qualitative, so it is likely that you will only need to focus on one of these chapters. However, some projects may utilise a mixed methods approach, encompassing elements of quantitative *and* qualitative research. It is important to understand in which cases it might be appropriate to apply both quantitative and qualitative research methodology within a single study. This chapter will provide an overview of mixed methods research and will provide some guidance to those of you ambitious enough to brave a mixed methods dissertation. You should use the information in this chapter in conjunction with the information in the previous two chapters.

Learning outcomes

By the end of this chapter you will:

- Understand what mixed methods research entails
- Understand some of the benefits and challenges to conducting mixed methods research
- Understand when it is appropriate to apply both quantitative *and* qualitative approaches to a single study
- Understand the unique characteristics of a mixed methods study, and how to sufficiently but concisely explain both the quantitative and the qualitative elements in your written report.

8.1 What is mixed methods research?

Mixed methods research is research that incorporates both quantitative *and* qualitative methodologies. This means that you will collect, analyse and report *both* quantitative (numerical) *and* qualitative ('wordy') data.

8.2 Benefits of mixed methods research

There are many benefits of conducting mixed methods research. For example, it can overcome some of the issues we might encounter with single method research projects by providing an insight into both statistical significance *and* participant accounts of the phenomenon under investigation. It allows for methodological diversity, encouraging consideration of multiple theoretical and practical approaches, and widening the focus of the research.

Conducting mixed methods research can allow you to follow up one methodology with further analysis using the alternative methodology – for example, it allows you to follow up quantitative research with further exploratory analysis into participants' lived experiences, broadening quantitative findings to take account of participants' dialogue or narrative. Alternatively, it gives you an opportunity to provide evidence of statistical significance to support the views of your participants, making the results more generalisable.

Taking all of the above into consideration, perhaps the greatest benefit of mixed methods research is that it provides us with a deeper and more thorough insight into the statistical and experiential accounts of the topic under investigation, compared to that which we would achieve through a single method alone. As such, this type of research often provides us with a more sophisticated understanding of the research topic, which can influence real-world policy and practice.

8.3 Challenges of mixed methods research

Above, we have discussed many of the benefits of conducting mixed methods research. However, it is also important to consider that there are many challenges when conducting this type of research, especially as a dissertation student. Firstly, mixed methods projects require you to be familiar and confident with both quantitative and qualitative designs, and this can put a strain on your ability as a researcher. When planning your project, you should consider your strengths to give you the best possible chance of success. If you do not feel confident or sufficiently able to address both types of methodology (e.g. if you feel that your ability is much weaker in one type of research than the other), you need to consider whether you are prepared to learn and invest time in developing your skills in both areas.

Secondly, mixed methods research is extremely time-consuming, as it requires you essentially to conduct two studies within one. There is the initial time commitment to educate yourself sufficiently about both types of research; the time commitment to conduct both quantitative (e.g. questionnaires or experiments) and qualitative (e.g. interviews or focus groups) methods; and the time commitment to analyse both types of data (understanding, conducting and interpreting your quantitative data analysis, and transcribing, analysing and extracting themes from your qualitative data), as well as then writing up both parts of your study and considering how they complement one another. You need to consider whether this is a commitment that you are willing to make as it is likely that a mixed methods study will require you to invest significantly more time than a single method project. Dissertation modules usually run for two academic terms, which means you are limited to some extent on time, so you will need to consider whether it is feasible for you to conduct this type of research within the scope of your dissertation module, or whether you are being unnecessarily overambitious. Discuss this with your supervisor if you are considering a mixed methods approach.

We must also consider the competing theoretical perspectives of quantitative and qualitative approaches. You will need to justify the inclusion of both parts of the design and to explain the findings of each method clearly in relation to research and theory – so you need to understand the different theoretical perspectives that might apply to each part of your study. Naturally, quantitative methods will lend themselves to very different theoretical perspectives than qualitative methods. Sometimes, these perspectives might contradict one another, and similarly, the results of the quantitative and qualitative parts of your study might not support one another as might be expected. You need to consider how you would explain this in relation to your own theoretical standpoint. Why have you chosen to conduct mixed methods research? What did you think you were going to find, and how did you anticipate that the two parts of the project would complement one another? How could your own theoretical perspective on the topic explain any differences in findings between the quantitative and qualitative aspects? How could the competing theoretical perspectives be explained or linked together in light of your findings? These are all questions that you will need to consider at some point during the conduct and write-up of your mixed methods project, so it is worth planning ahead and thinking about this from the beginning.

8.4 So why (and when) should you choose a mixed methods approach?

Taking the above challenges and obstacles into consideration, why (and when) should you choose to employ a mixed methods approach? Well, if we return to the idea that your methodology needs to be mapped onto your research question, you should carefully consider whether your research question merits investigation via multiple methods. Of course, you may have more than one research question, and each may lend itself to different methods, but the key here is *justification* – you need to be able to justify every decision you make when designing and conducting your study. So, put simply, it is only worth employing mixed methods if you can justify a clear reason why this might be necessary to fully answer your research question or to address your aims.

Secondly, you need to consider whether your knowedge and skills and the remit of your dissertation module permit you to embark on the journey of designing and conducting a mixed methods study. As discussed above, mixed methods research requires you to be familiar and confident with both types of research, so ask yourself whether you can succeed in both areas – if you are in doubt, is it worth the risk? Similarly, you need to consider whether it is realistic and feasible for you to conduct a mixed methods project within the scope of your dissertation module.

Three important questions to ask yourself when deciding whether to use a mixed methods approach are as follows:

1. Would a mixed methods approach help you to answer your research question more fully? Would a mixed methods approach add important or insightful data to your project in comparison to a single method approach?
2. Are you able and confident enough to attempt both methods within your project?
3. Is it feasible for you to conduct a mixed methods study within the scope of your dissertation module? Do you have the time and resources necessary to attempt both approaches?

If the answer to all of these questions is 'yes', a mixed methods approach may be appropriate. If you answered 'no' to any of these questions, discuss your ideas with your supervisor to determine whether it is worth considering a mixed methods approach or not.

8.5 Reporting mixed methods research design

The key thing to remember when reporting mixed methods research is that you need to report the details of both the quantitative and the qualitative parts of the design. In your methodology chapter, you will need to explain concisely the importance, relevance and rationale of each part of the study, and how they complement or extend one another. You are essentially reporting two studies within one – so with the design, participants, materials and procedure, you will need to take account of both the obvious and subtle differences between the quantitative and qualitative parts. It is likely that you will have far fewer participants in the qualitative part of your study than in the quantitative part, so you will need to explain both of your samples, as well as the different procedures that participants will be involved in during each part of the study. In the materials section, you will need to explain the selection of quantitative measures as well as the development of qualitative materials such as your interview schedule. As such, the methodology chapter for a mixed methods project will be substantially lengthier than a project utilising a single method approach.

Chapter summary

Mixed methods research combines aspects of both quantitative and qualitative research design. This chapter has outlined the benefits and challenges of conducting mixed methods research, and discussed when it might be appropriate to do so, as well as outlining some key questions to ask yourself when considering a mixed methods approach.

You should use the information in this chapter in conjunction with the information provided in Chapters 6 and 7.

Checklist

✓   Consider how mixed methodology might benefit your project, and how it might help to answer your research question(s). Consider the challenges, too, and whether a mixed methods project is both worthwhile and feasible within the scope of your dissertation module.

✓   Book an appointment with your supervisor to discuss the possibility of conducting a mixed methods project.

✓   Re-read Chapters 6 and 7 to determine which quantitative and qualitative methods you might use in your mixed methods study.

9

Ethical Considerations

All psychological research projects must abide by the ethical guidelines and principles set out by the British Psychological Society. Before you can collect any data for your dissertation, you will need to obtain ethical approval from your institution's appropriate research ethics committee. This chapter will discuss ethical concerns, which you will need to consider when planning and conducting your project. For more guidance, you are advised to refer to the British Psychological Society's (2018) *Code of Ethics and Conduct*.

Learning outcomes

By the end of this chapter you will:

- Understand the importance of research ethics
- Understand the main ethical principles relevant to working with human participants
- Be able to make ethical decisions regarding the design and conduct of your project
- Understand how to protect the welfare of both your participants and yourself as the researcher
- Understand how to ethically collect and store your research data
- Know how to prepare ethical documents, including your participant information sheet/ briefing form, consent form and debrief.

9.1 An introduction to research ethics

The importance of research ethics in the planning and execution of scientific research should not be underestimated. It is a common misconception that ethical principles are separate from the planning of a research project, when in practice the two processes should be considered simultaneously. In fact, ethical principles should be taken into consideration at *all stages* of the research process, from planning your research design and methodology, to working with your participants, to analysing and storing your data. As a psychological researcher, you have a moral responsibility and professional obligation to uphold the ethical principles set out by the British Psychological Society at all times. Your understanding and consideration of these principles in the planning of your project will usually be monitored by your institution through an ethics review process. What we mean by this is that before you collect any data for your dissertation, you will need to obtain ethical approval from your institution's appropriate research ethics committee or board by submitting an ethical approval application form for review. *You* are responsible for obtaining ethical approval for your project and must not collect any data until this approval has been granted.

Top tip!

> Consider ethical principles at all stages of the research process, from planning your research design and methodology, to working with your participants, to analysing and storing your data. Don't wait to think about ethics when it comes to completing your ethical approval application!

Throughout this chapter, we will discuss the main ethical concerns you need to consider when planning and conducting your project. For more guidance, you are advised to refer to the British Psychological Society's (2018) *Code of Ethics and Conduct*. Importantly, whilst codes of ethical conduct such as this are important in our understanding of ethical principles, they are not intended simply to provide a set of rules or regulations for researchers to follow. Instead, they should be used to promote moral and ethical thinking, behaviour, attitudes and judgements, such that you are able to understand how to apply these principles not only to your current project but to all work you undertake.

EMPLOYABILITY TIP!

Being able to think ethically about your work is a key employability skill – it shows that you can reflect on your practice and think about how to protect both yourself and those you are working with.

9.2 The ethical review process

9.2.1 Why do we need to apply for ethical approval?

As a student, you have a responsibility to abide by your insitution's ethical guidelines. Every time you conduct a research project, whether as an undergraduate, postgraduate, member of a research team or academic staff member, you will need to submit an ethical approval application to your institution's relevant research ethics committee. This is so that your institution can monitor the research that is being conducted by staff and students, and can be sure that such research adheres to ethical principles. You also need to consider the reputation of the wider department in which you are studying, your research group (if you are part of one), your supervisor, and the organisation in which you plan to collect your data.

The ethical application process is an important part of the dissertation project, because you cannot collect data without prior ethical approval. You need data in order to complete your dissertation, and you need to complete your dissertation in order to complete your course. If we conduct research incorrectly and don't adhere to ethical principles, there may also be legal implications. You need to consider all of these issues when completing your application and address any that may arise before beginning the data collection process – for example, how you will protect your participants from any risk of psychological or physical harm that could arise as a result of them taking part in the research. However, ethics isn't just about protecting the participant – it is also about protecting you as the researcher, and ethical approval plays an important role in ensuring your own safety during the research process.

EMPLOYABILITY TIP!

If you plan to go on to study at postgraduate level, or engage in further research in the future, being able to demonstrate a thorough understanding of research ethics will be really important. As mentioned earlier, you should think about ethics throughout the planning process, not just when it comes to preparing for data collection.

9.2.2 What happens during the ethical review process?

You should work with your supervisor to make sure that your application is clear and that you have fully explained all considerations. Remember that you will need to obtain ethical approval before you begin collecting data, so you need to start thinking about this early on. Many institutions require you to have your application signed off by your supervisor prior to you submitting it for approval, so it is worth discussing your project and the ethical considerations of your research in detail with your supervisor.

Once you submit your ethical approval application form to the relevant research ethics committee or board at your institution, it will be reviewed and commented on by relevant reviewers. Based on the content of your application and the comments of the reviewer(s), the ethics committee will then make a decision on whether to grant ethical approval for your study or not. Approval may depend on certain conditions being met or points being clarified, for example if something is unclear in your original application or if the reviewers or members of the committee have further questions about your project. You can only begin collecting data once full approval has been granted (i.e. once the committee is satisfied that you have met all ethical principles fully and have answered all questions completely and satisfactorily).

9.3 An overview of ethical principles and laws

There are certain principles that we need to adhere to when applying for ethical approval and conducting the research. These principles are often defined by the relevant regulatory body – in psychology these principles are outlined by the British Psychological Society (BPS). The BPS (2014) *Code of Human Research Ethics* sets out the general principles that are applicable to all research contexts and are intended to cover all research with human participants. The Code explains that researchers should respect the rights and dignity of participants in their research and the legitimate interests of stakeholders by adhering to certain principles. It is also important to recognise that internet-mediated research is becoming more and more popular. If you wish to conduct your research online, the BPS has produced some newer guidelines for internet-mediated research (BPS, 2017).

In addition to the BPS Codes, you should also consider professional legislation. The Data Protection Act 2018 is one example. It relates to the storage and protection of data, such as the personal information of your participants and the data you have obtained from them. The Safeguarding Vulnerable Groups Act 2006 is relevant to participants who may be part of a vulnerable group, such as those with disabilities, or children and young people. If you are conducting research that involves contact with children or vulnerable adults, you will need to go through a checking and barring process first (via the Disclosure and Barring Service (DBS) in England and Wales, Disclosure Scotland or Access Northern Ireland).

9.4 Recruitment and treatment of participants

The British Psychological Society (2014) states that psychologists and researchers should consider all research from the perspective of the participants, for the purpose of eliminating potential risks to psychological wellbeing, physical health, personal values or dignity. We will discuss consideration of potential risks later in this chapter, but first it is important to think about how you will approach and recruit your participants, and to ensure that recruitment is conducted ethically. In doing so, there are a number of concepts of recruitment that need to be considered, which are discussed in detail below.

9.4.1 Inclusion and exclusion criteria

Firstly, consider who your participants will be – who are you planning to target? Are there any requirements for participation? Any characteristics that potential participants must possess in order to participate in the study are called **inclusion criteria**. For example, if you are planning to investigate the experiences of teachers of SEN children, your inclusion criteria must include that 'participants must be teachers of SEN children'. You should also consider whether there are any confounding variables that could affect your results, or anything that could have a detrimental effect on your participants' welfare. Any characteristics that you *do not* want your participants to possess (i.e. any criteria that might mean a particular person should *not* take part in the research) are called **exclusion criteria**.

Inclusion and exclusion criteria need to be outlined in your ethical approval application. This is important because if you do not identify at this point why particular individuals might be excluded from participating, you could be accused of discriminating against potential participants on the basis of characteristics that were not identified in the planning of the project.

It is especially important to recognise that certain individuals may be particularly vulnerable in certain studies. For example, someone who has had an eating disorder may be excluded from a study on eating behaviour, or someone who has a severe mental health condition may be excluded from a study on depression. These individuals may be excluded to protect them from potential psychological harm as a result of taking part in the research. Although researchers do sometimes conduct research with such vulnerable groups, the ethical implications of these participants taking part in the study may be extremely complex, particularly for an undergraduate study, and would not be advised at this level. Similarly, groups that could systematically bias the findings of the study may also be excluded. For example, people who have a specific developmental disability may be excluded as they might perform differently from a normally developing population on particular tasks and may not give an accurate representation of the expected level of performance. It is important that you consider all potential issues with the recruitment of certain individuals, the impact that recruitment could have on your study in general and on the resulting data. The inclusion and exclusion criteria that you identify will need to be listed in your participant consent form to ensure that your participants understand what criteria they must meet in order to take part.

9.4.2 Advertisement and initial recruitment of potential participants

Once you have identified who your participants will be, you also need to consider how these participants will be recruited. Consider whether and how you will advertise your study and through what means. Will you advertise online? Use a poster? Advertise on your university campus? How will you word your advertisement? Your institution's ethics committee may require you to attach a copy of any advertisement to your ethical approval application or, at the very least, your supervisor will need to approve such advertisements before they go live. Some guidance on creating an advertisement for participants is provided in Figure 9.1.

Guidance on recruitment posters/advertisements

- As a minimum, posters should include:
  - Brief study description
  - Inclusion criteria (exclusion criteria can also be included; however, proper consideration should be given to how these are worded to ensure they are not discriminatory)
  - Name and course of student
  - Student email address
  - Details on how to sign up
  - Date by which study is to be completed (and advertisement will be taken down)
- Ensure that posters contain enough detail for potential participants to understand but not so much that they do not read the content.

Figure 9.1   Guidance on creating an advertisement for participants

Next, consider how you will approach participants, and what your sampling technique will be. Different recruitment methods may be relevant to different types of projects – to help you decide what is most appropriate for you, some of the most popular sampling techniques are explained in section 6.6.2.

9.4.3 Informed consent

Ensuring that participants have the capacity to provide informed consent is one of the most important principles for ensuring the safety and welfare of your participants. Indeed, the British Psychological Society state that we must 'ensure that participants from vulnerable populations (such as children, persons lacking capacity, and those in a dependent or unequal relationship) are given ample opportunity to understand the nature, purpose and anticipated outcomes of any research participation, so that they may give consent to the extent that their capabilities allow' (British Psychological Society, 2014, p. 31). In order to do so, your participants must be fully informed of the nature of the study (using a briefing sheet or participant information sheet), they must have the opportunity to ask questions (to clarify any points they are unsure of) and must be asked to sign a formal consent form (to document their consent to participate). Before asking individuals to sign the consent form, explain that their participation in the research is entirely voluntary. In addition, be clear that they are free to withdraw from the study at any time (before, during or after their participation, up to a given date), that withdrawing from the study will have no negative consequences for them and that any data collected from them up to that point will be destroyed. If you are unsure as to whether any/all of these points are relevant or true to your study, we would advise that you discuss the ethical requirements with your supervisor as soon as possible.

The briefing sheet, or participant information sheet, should therefore contain (as a minimum) the following:

- Information about the background and purpose of the research
- Details of who is organising and conducting the research
- Confirmation of ethical approval for the research
- What participants will be expected to do, and how long participation is likely to last
- Confirmation that participation is voluntary and that participants have the right to withdraw at any point before, during or after their participation up to a given date, along with details of *how* to withdraw from the research
- Information about any risks and benefits of taking part, and details of relevant sources of further support
- What will happen to participants' data, who will have access to it and how they can find out more about the study findings
- Contact information for you and your supervisor.

See our online resources for a full template (a section of which is depicted in Figure 9.2).

PARTICIPANT INFORMATION SHEET

STUDY TITLE HERE

STUDY BACKGROUND
You are being asked to take part in a research study on…

WHAT YOU ARE BEING ASKED TO DO
If you decide to take part in this study, you will be asked to…

WHAT ARE THE RISKS AND BENEFITS OF TAKING PART?
Consider the psychological and/or physical risks to participants, e.g. if a sensitive subject, could they become distressed? You will need to explain these risks here and how they will be mitigated. If no obvious risks, state the following: There are no specific risks to this study over and above those experienced in everyday encounters.

If there is an incentive for taking part, mention it here. If not, state the following: Whilst there are no direct benefits of taking part, it is hoped that this study will advance knowledge in…

YOUR RIGHT TO WITHDRAW AND WITHHOLD INFORMATION
In line with the regulations outlined by the British Psychological Society, you can stop being a part of the research study at any time without explanation. You are still entitled to the same benefits as an individual who completes the study. You can also have your data withdrawn from the time you complete until [*insert date: this should be a date that allows you sufficient time to analyse your data before the submission deadline*], by which time your data will have been analysed and written up. Please see contact details below if you wish to withdraw. During the study, you also have the right to omit or refuse to answer or respond to any question that is asked of you.

Figure 9.2   Example section of participant information sheet

As a researcher, it is your responsibility to ensure that you obtain and retain adequate records of participant consent, including details of *when* and *how* each participant has provided consent to participate (British Psychological Society, 2014). As such, once participants have been fully briefed about the study, you will usually need to obtain written consent (or an electronic version if you are conducting an online study), confirming not only that participants consent to participate, but also that they understand the nature of the study (Figure 9.3). The consent form should therefore contain the following as a minimum:

- Brief reiteration of the aims and nature of the study
- Check boxes or statements for participants to confirm that they understand:
   o   The information provided in the briefing form/participant information sheet
   o   The inclusion/exclusion criteria for the research
   o   That participation is entirely voluntary and that they have the right to withdraw from the research at any point before, during or after their participation up to a given date
- Space for the participant to sign and date the form (if a hard copy) or a check box for participants to confirm that they agree to participate in the research (if an online study)
- Space for the participant unique reference code (if a hard copy)

PARTICIPANT CONSENT FORM

STUDY TITLE HERE

BRIEF SUMMARY OF PROJECT
Provide a brief summary of the project

In order to participate in this study, we need to ensure that you understand the nature of the research, as outlined in the participant information sheet. Please tick the boxes to indicate that you understand and agree to the following conditions:

I confirm that I have read the participant information sheet for this study. I have had the opportunity to consider the information, ask questions and have had these answered satisfactorily. ☐

I understand that in order to take part in this study, I should/should NOT be [*place inclusion/exclusion criteria here [e.g. at least 18 years old*] ☐

I understand that personal data about me will be collected for the purposes of the research study including [*insert appropriate personal details, e.g. name, date of birth, ethnicity, sexuality, audio recordings, etc.*], and that these will be processed in accordance with data protection regulations. ☐

I understand that my participation is voluntary and that I am free to withdraw at any time without giving any reason, without my rights being affected. ☐

I understand that my data is anonymous and will be stored on secure university servers. I understand that it will only be used by the investigators for research purposes and that there is a possibility this research will be presented at conferences or published in journal publications. ☐

I understand that the audio from this interview will be recorded via Dictaphone. (*For interview studies only – delete if this does not apply*) ☐

I agree to take part in this study. ☐

_____   _____
Participant's name (printed)   **Researcher's name (printed)**

_____   _____
Participant's signature   **Researcher's signature**

_____   _____
Date   **Date**

Figure 9.3   Example consent form

If your participants are under the age of 18, or belong to any vulnerable groups, you must address the briefing form and consent form to the parent or legal guardian of the potential participant rather than the participant themselves. This ensures that consent is provided by a responsible adult. However, the process of working with participants of this nature is often more complex than simply gaining parental consent, and this is something that you should discuss with your supervisor when planning and conducting your project. You should also follow this by seeking assent (agreement to participate from someone who cannot give legal consent) from the participant themselves – this can often be achieved through the use of a verbal assent form (Figure 9.4) which is read aloud to the participant, giving them an opportunity to accept or decline to participate.

PARTICIPANT VERBAL ASSENT FORM

To be read aloud to child participants

'Hello [participant's name], my name is [name] and I would like to do some [type of activity] activities with you. There are [number of activities] activities for you to take part in and it should take no longer than [number of minutes] minutes. Your parents/guardians and your head teacher have given permission for you to do these activities with me.

Would you like to do these activities? **YES/NO**

If you decide that you want to stop at any point, just say you would like to stop and you can go back to class.

Figure 9.4   Example verbal assent form

9.4.4 Deception

Wherever possible, you should ensure that your participants are fully informed of the nature and aims of the research prior to their participation so that they are able to provide informed consent. As such, the deliberate deception of participants should be avoided wherever possible. However, in some research situations, it is not possible to fully inform the participants about the true nature of the research project prior to their participation to avoid risking the validity of the data. For example, if your study involves priming participants, and they know they are going to be primed, this could influence the findings. In such cases, a distinction can be made between withholding information regarding the research questions and hypotheses of the study, and deliberately misleading participants. Specific information surrounding the aims and research questions can be retained to avoid revealing the true nature of the variables being studied and giving participants an opportunity to alter their behaviour or responses to conform with demand characteristics or social desirability. In such cases, this information must be revealed to participants immediately following their participation and the true nature of the study should be fully explained. At this point, participants must again be informed of their right to withdraw from the study and have their data destroyed.

9.4.5 Debriefing

Following participation, it is important that you recognise your ongoing responsibility towards your participants. You should offer them the opportunity to ask any questions they have about the research and what will happen with their data, remind them of their right to withdraw themselves and their data from the study at any point up to a given date, and provide them with your contact details should they wish to contact you for further information, to withdraw, or to find out about the findings of the study at a later date. You can do this through a debriefing form or letter (Figure 9.5), or in person at a debriefing session. Regardless of format, debriefing should include the following as a minimum requirement:

- Thanks to the participant(s) for taking part in the research
- Reiteration of the aims and purpose of the research
- Further information about the background and rationale for the research, and how the findings might be applied to enhance knowledge or inform practice in the specified area
- Contact details for you and your supervisor
- Details of how participants can obtain further information about the findings of the study
- Details of relevant sources of support for participants following participation
- A reminder that participants can withdraw their data at any point up to a given date, by which time their data will have been analysed.

DEBRIEFING SHEET

STUDY TITLE HERE

SUMMARY OF PROJECT
Thank participants for taking part. Provide a summary of the project **in terms understandable to a layperson**, *including a brief description of the background and overview of what the study involved. Explain the nature of any deception, why it was necessary and discuss the potential implications.*

FURTHER GUIDANCE
Provide guidance relating to any negative implications arising from the project – e.g. contact details of relevant support services.

KEEPING IN TOUCH
Reiterate details of what will happen next with the data. Remind participants that they have the right to withdraw up to a given date. Provide instructions on how to withdraw from the study. If they created an anonymous code as part of their participation, this will be needed to withdraw them from the study.

ANY MORE QUESTIONS?
If you have any further questions, please contact the researcher(s) using the details below.

Please provide your contact details and your supervisor's.

If you are unhappy at any point in the study, or if there is a problem, please contact the [*provide details of the relevant research ethics committee*].

Figure 9.5   Example debriefing sheet

9.4.6 Right to withdraw

The right to withdraw has been mentioned above in relation to the participant information sheet, consent form and debrief, as this right should be fully explained on each of these participant-facing documents. As a researcher, you have a responsibility to make sure that your participants understand this right to withdraw from the study at any point before, during or after their participation, and up to a given date. It is important that you identify a specific date by which participants must withdraw if they wish to do so, because at some point you will need to analyse your data. If you do not identify a cut-off date for withdrawal, you could encounter issues if a participant approaches you to withdraw their data after the data have already been analysed – this may mean that you have to revisit the raw data, withdraw a participant's responses and re-analyse the data, which is a time-consuming and effortful process. It is usual to allow one or two weeks after participation for participants to withdraw, but check require-ments with your supervisor/department/ethics board first.

You should make it clear to participants that their participation is entirely volun-tary and that withdrawing from the study will have no negative consequences for them. In the event that participation involves a reward or incentive for par-ticipants, those who withdraw from the study should still be entitled to the same benefits as those whose data remain part of the study.

Participants may withdraw from a research project for a variety of reasons. Before participation, they may change their mind once they learn about the requirements for participation, or they may have needed to ask additional ques-tions to decide whether or not they wanted to take part. Once these questions have been answered and they learn more about what they will be asked to do, they may decide that they do not want to take part. This might be due, for example, to the nature of the research, the topic being studied or their ability to invest the required time. Additionally, the inclusion criteria may not have been obvious to participants on initial advertisements, and they may later realise that they do not meet the eligibility criteria. Alternatively, participants might have an ethical, moral, religious or personal preference regarding exposure to certain stimuli, materials or experimental conditions. It is imperative that you treat all participants with dignity and that you respect any decision to withdraw. Participants should not be asked to disclose their reason for withdrawing from a research project, and it should be clear to them on the participant-facing documentation that they do not have to give any explanation for their decision to withdraw.

As well as the participant actively deciding to withdraw from the research, you should also consider what actions *you* will take if a participant becomes distressed or uncomfortable within the research environment. Consider how you would identify that a participant might have lost the capacity to consent to taking part, and how you would respond to this situation. For example, if you were working with child participants, you would need to consider the types of behaviour that might characterise a child no longer wanting to continue with the research activity. It is important that you understand how to detect this because young children often don't feel comfortable about not cooperating with an adult's requests, particularly in a school setting. The child being timid or uncharacteristically quiet, and behaviours such as fidgeting, becoming distracted or changing the topic of conversation may indicate that the child does not want to continue. Alternatively, if you are researching a sensitive topic, there is a possibility that individuals may become distressed or upset as a result of their participation.

If any of the above scenarios occur during the process of data collection, you will need to decide whether to offer the affected participant the option to withdraw from the research environment. In making this decision, it is important to consider whether distress is an expected part of your study design (e.g. if you are using a stressor task to purposefully inflict stress upon your participants), or whether distress was a highly likely outcome due to the nature of the project (e.g. in a project investigating themes of distress). If you are not expecting participants to experience distress during your study, or if a participant experiences an unusually high level of distress, you must recognise that you have an ethical responsibility to remove them from the research environment. In this case, any data already collected from them should be destroyed. The participant should be provided with information on sources of additional support, and in the case of working with children or other vulnerable groups of participants, the relevant safeguarding procedures should be followed to ensure that the individual is protected from any long-lasting negative effects of distress caused by participation.

9.4.7 Minimising and mitigating potential risks

One of the most important parts of the ethical review process is addressing the concept of risk. It is important to address potential risks in line with the relevant standards of practice outlined by the BPS, such as duty of care and respect for the participants' confidentiality and privacy (confidentiality will be discussed further in section 9.5.1). As a researcher, you will need to identify and minimise any physical and psychological risks both to the participants and to yourself as the researcher (and other members of the research team if relevant). It is important to recognise that there is never no risk at all – there is always some risk, no matter how small. If you cannot identify any significant risk, you should state that the risk of physical and/or psychological harm is minimal, and you should justify *why*. Alternatively, if you *can* identify any substantial risks (physical or psychological) you should explain what precautions you will take to minimise these risks.

When you apply for ethical approval for your study, it is important that you are able to identify what the risks might be, and consider what you will do to minimise the possibility of any risk occurring and how you will minimise any negative or long-lasting impact for the participant and/or the researcher. For example, are there services or resources that your participants (and you) could be referred to for further support if they feel uncomfortable or distressed as a result of the study? There is always a risk that participants may feel uncomfortable with some of the topics discussed or assessed in your study, particularly if you are conducting research on a sensitive subject. Issues such as death, crime, personal health and safety, amongst other issues, may arise during the course of your project, and you will need to explain what you will do to minimise the risks to participants' psychological health – for example, by fully explaining the topic beforehand, ensuring that participants are aware of the risk before agreeing to participate and ensuring that you provide appropriate information on sources of further support.

You should follow the same process for evaluating personal risk to yourself as a researcher. It would be advisable to avoid conducting your research project on a topic that is likely to be highly distressing to you – for example, studying depression if you suffer from mental health issues yourself. However, even when avoiding such topics, there is always some potential risk to you as a researcher. For example, there is the risk of how a participant may respond to your study. In your ethics application, you will need to explain how you will protect yourself from physical and psychological harm as a researcher – for example, by conducting your data collection in a public space or on a university campus during daylight hours, and by being aware of the support services available to you as a student at the university. It is important to consider the research environment and how to protect yourself (and the wider research team, if relevant) in the ethics application, because your institution has a duty of care to you as a researcher, and, as such, the ethics committee will not let you do anything that could put you in danger. For this reason, if you make any changes to your study after gaining ethical approval – for example, if you decide to conduct your research in a different environment – you will need to submit an ethics amendment to the committee so that it can assess the changes.

9.4.8 Vulnerable groups

You should consider how you will be interacting with the participants in your study; for example, if you are working with children (anyone under the age of 18) or vulnerable adults. You should consider how you will minimise any risks that may arise from working with such groups, and how you will protect both your participants and yourself as the researcher. If you declare that you will be working with any vulnerable groups, you will need to apply in advance for a DBS check (in England and Wales), or a Disclosure Scotland or Access Northern Ireland check. If you are planning to go into an external organisation to collect your data – for example, a school – you also need to provide an indication that you are allowed to collect data there by providing evidence of gatekeeper permission. This will normally be provided in the form of a letter explaining that the organisation has approved your study and that they are happy for you to collect your data with them (Figure 9.6).

> DEAR [STUDENT NAME]
>
> I am writing to confirm that I am happy for you to conduct your research project, [project name here] within our organisation in [month, year]. Please send me some further information when you can.
>
> Best wishes,
>
> [gatekeeper name]
> [gatekeeper position within organisation]

Figure 9.6   Example gatekeeper permission letter

9.5 Data protection

As well as ensuring that your participants are fully informed about your research, you need to consider how you will protect the details of your participants in line with the Data Protection Act 2018. This is both an ethical and legal requirement.

9.5.1 Anonymity and confidentiality

When you collect and report research data, you need to ensure that participants are anonymous, or that the data are confidential at the very least. A lot of people get confused between these two terms and use the terms interchangeably, so let us explain the difference:

- **Anonymity**: This is when even you as a researcher won't be able to identify an individual participant and that participant's responses. There *are* ways to make the data completely anonymous, but the problem is that if the participant is completely anonymous, they will not be able to withdraw their data as you will not be able to identify them or their data. Because of the ethical implications, most people will go with confidentiality rather than complete anonymity.

- **Confidentiality**: The best way to ensure confidentiality is to provide participants with a participant code or number, or a way of creating one, so that their names will not be recorded anywhere other than on the consent form. This way, if you need to locate the data of an individual participant (e.g. if they contact you later and want to withdraw), you can go back to the data set and find it using the code or number on their consent form. Remember that regardless of whether you use this method or not, the consent forms and raw data need to be stored separately and securely.

If you are conducting qualitative research – for example if you want to interview participants about their experiences or opinions about a particular phenomenon – you can ensure confidentiality by providing a pseudonym for participants. It is important *never* to record participants' real names at any point during transcription, and also to either retract or provide pseudonyms for the names of other people or organisations that may be mentioned during the interview(s).

9.6 Research publication

At this stage, it is worth thinking ahead to the future – if you are considering publication of your dissertation, you will need to ensure that you account for this in your ethics application. This is important because you need to gain approval to share the findings of the research (and in many cases the data) outside of the dissertation module. The possibility of publication will need to be communicated to your participants so that they are informed of how the data they provide may be used, so you'll also need to include a statement to this effect within your participant-facing documents. You should discuss other requirements for publication ethics with your supervisor, who will be able to advise regarding your institution's specific requirements.

Homework

Locate a copy of your relevant university research ethics application form and read through the relevant advice above in relation to each section of the form. Start to make some notes on each section in relation to the advice provided in this chapter.

Chapter summary

Ethical approval is a moral, legal and professional obligation of all researchers and you must adhere to the principles set out by the British Psychological Society at all times.

You will need to apply for ethical approval from your relevant university ethics board and obtain full ethical approval for your study before you will be permitted to begin data collection.

In this chapter, we have considered some general principles of ethical research, which you will need to consider when planning, conducting and writing up your dissertation research project.

Checklist

✓ Read and understand the general ethical principles outlined in this chapter and in the British Psychological Society's Code of Conduct.

✓ Download a copy of your relevant university or department research ethics application.

✓ Start making notes on your ethical approval application form in relation to the advice presented in this chapter.

✓ Book an appointment with your supervisor to discuss any of the sections of the form that you do not fully understand.

DATA ANALYSIS

By this stage in your project, you will have designed your study, gained ethical approval and collected your data. The next step will be to decide on the most appropriate data analysis strategy to use to analyse your data, to conduct your data analysis, and to interpret and report your findings. This part will discuss both quantitative and qualitative data analysis, in the light of information provided in Part 2 on Methodology. It would be impossible for us to fully cover all methods of data analysis in this part of the textbook, so you should use the information provided here in conjunction with your research methods material from earlier in your course.

10

Quantitative Data Analysis

Once you have collected the data for your project, the next step will be to prepare for data analysis. This chapter will guide you through the preparation of quantitative data and will recap on some of the information from your research methods modules earlier in your course. It would be impossible for us to cover every method of data analysis in sufficient detail here, so it is important that you also refer to your course material on research methods when conducting your data analysis and writing up your results. This chapter will guide you in identifying the most appropriate method of quantitative data analysis for your study, as well as setting up your data file in SPSS and writing a generic results chapter for your dissertation.

Learning outcomes

By the end of this chapter you will:

- Understand the steps in preparing for data analysis
- Understand your variables and your data
- Understand how your research question(s) and methodology can help you to identify the most appropriate statistical test for your data
- Understand parametric assumptions
- Understand the components of a standard quantitative results chapter.

10.1 Managing your data

Before you can begin to think about preparing for data analysis, you need to understand your data, and in order to be able to understand your data, you need to be able to manage it effectively – both during the data collection process and after.

It is likely that you will have a lot of data if you are conducting a quantitative study – after all, to achieve power in your analysis you will need to ensure that you have collected data from a sufficient number of participants. As such, it is important to keep your data safe and organised throughout the data collection process. If you are conducting an online study – for example by using online survey software such as Survey Monkey, Qualtrics or Google Forms – your data will already be in electronic form. If you are conducting a face-to-face study, it is likely that you will have hard copies of your data, whether in questionnaires, tests or measures. This data will need to be translated into electronic form so that it can be entered into data analysis software such as SPSS. In doing so, you will need to understand how to score your data, transforming score sheets or survey answers into numerical data. Once you have scored your data (see section 10.1.1), you can begin inputting your data to your statistical analysis software (see section 10.3).

10.1.1 Scoring your data: Standardised assessments

If you are conducting a study using standardised tests or measures of particular abilities, the test should come with standardised instructions on how to score the data. Commonly, you need to take into consideration standardised scoring, which requires more than simply totalling the score from a particular scale. For example, if you are conducting a test of cognitive ability in children, you would usually need firstly to total their score and then use a standardised scoring table to convert the total raw score into a standardised score – taking the child's age into consideration. Understanding standardised scoring is important because standardised scores are more reliable than raw scores as they take into consideration where we would expect a child to be on the scale (i.e. what we would expect them to score) at a particular age. For this reason, it is important to take note of children's ages (usually in months) when collecting your data – but make sure you store this information securely in accordance with data protection regulations. Many ability tests will have specific instructions for calculating standardised scores, so it is particularly important to consult the instruction manual for the test(s) you are using both before data collection (so that you can ensure that you run the test correctly and collect the required information from your participants) and during the scoring process (to ensure that you score, convert and record your data correctly).

10.1.2 Scoring your data: Questionnaires and surveys (Likert scales)

If you are conducting a questionnaire study, responses could come in many different forms. One of the most widely used quantitative response methods is the Likert scale (Likert, 1932). A Likert scale is effective for measuring your participants' responses on a scale from 0 or 1 to X, where X can be any number depending on how many options you wish to give. This could help you to measure participants' level of agreement with a particular statement, or how positive or negative they feel about something. Depending on the wording of your questions/statements in the survey, you might need to reverse score some of your items. This will be relevant if some of your statements are positive and some are negative. For example, in Rosenberg's Self-Esteem Scale (1965) (Figure 10.1), statements 1, 2, 4, 6 and 7 are positive (meaning that a higher level of agreement would indicate a higher level of self-esteem) whereas statements 3, 5, 8, 9 and 10 are negative (meaning that a higher level of agreement would indicate a lower level of self-esteem). These negative items would therefore need to be reverse scored to take account of this in the scoring. So, if you have a four-point Likert scale, as in this example, you would allocate scores of 1, 2, 3 or 4 to each statement depending on the answer given. In the positive items, you would allocate a score of 4 to 'strongly agree' and a score of 1 to 'strongly disagree', whereas for the negative items you would allocate a score of 1 to 'strongly agree' and a score of 4 to 'strongly disagree'. The total score for the questionnaire (i.e. the total scores for all statements) would indicate the participant's level of self-esteem – the higher the score, the higher the self-esteem.

STATEMENT	Strongly Agree	Agree	Disagree	Strongly Disagree
1. I feel that I am a person of worth, at least on an equal plane with others.	O	O	O	O
2. I feel that I have a number of good qualities.	O	O	O	O
3. All in all, I am inclined to feel that I am a failure.	O	O	O	O
4. I am able to do things as well as most other people.	O	O	O	O
5. I feel I do not have much to be proud of.	O	O	O	O
6. I take a positive attitude toward myself.	O	O	O	O
7. On the whole, I am satisfied with myself.	O	O	O	O
8. I wish I could have more respect for myself.	O	O	O	O
9. I certainly feel useless at times.	O	O	O	O
10. At times I think I am no good at all.	O	O	O	O

Figure 10.1   Rosenberg's (1965) Self-Esteem Scale

Whilst we are discussing Likert Scales, it is important to consider how many items you have included on the scale and what impact this might have on participants' responses. This will help you to understand your data and might be something that you want to discuss when it comes to writing your disscussion chapter. One consideration is whether to have an odd or an even number of possible responses on the scale. If your scale has an odd number of response options, you are giving your participants the option to either agree or disagree, or to 'sit on the fence' in the middle, not committing to any level of agreement and providing a neutral response. This can be of benefit or hinderance to the data, because, whilst in many instances a neutral response may be relevant to participants' experiences or feelings towards a particular statement, it also often means that we can't decipher whether participants just can't decide or simply have no opinion on the statement, or whether they actually agree or disagree but are choosing not to commit. When you design your study, you should consider whether providing a neutral response option for participants might be relevant and useful. This largely depends on the topic area you are researching, how your questions or statements are worded and what population you are working with, so speak to your supervisor if you are unsure. If you choose not to provide a neutral option and your scale has an even number of response options, you are effectively presenting participants with 'forced choice' statements, where they have to decide whether they agree or disagree (but to varying extents). If we consider the example in Figure 10.1, the four response options mean that participants have to decide whether they agree or disagree with each statement, and then whether their agreement or disagreement could be classed as 'strong' or not. They have no option here to provide a neutral response, which, as discussed above, can be either of benefit or hindrance to the data, depending on the topic studied and what you want to find out from your participants.

10.2 Understanding your variables and which type of analysis you should use

Once you have scored your data, you are almost ready to begin setting up your data spreadsheet in preparation for data analysis. Throughout this chapter, we will refer to the use of SPSS, but you might also want to consider using an alternative statistical analysis package such as R. Your supervisor will be able to provide advice on which package is most suitable for your data – but most undergraduate courses will expect students to use SPSS as standard.

The first step in setting up your spreadsheet will be to understand your variables, because you will need to consider how to set up the Variable View page (Figure 10.2).

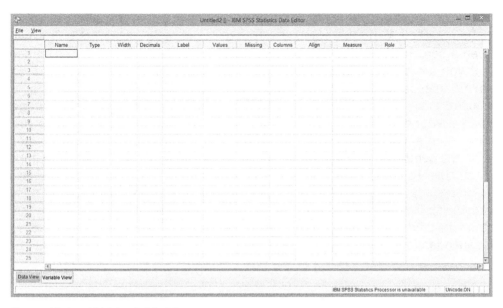

Figure 10.2   SPSS Variable View

In the first column of Variable View, you will see space to list your variable names. It is important to give your variables names that make sense and that you will remember, but also names that distinguish them from other variables. Also note that, in SPSS, your variable names cannot contain any spaces, so for example if you want to name a variable 'Time 1 score', you would need to use something like 'T1score' or 'Time1_score'. Within Variable View, you can also assign labels to your variables using the 'Label' column (5th column). This is useful if, for example, you have given a name to a variable and want it labelled in a different way within your output. Unlike variable names, labels *can* contain spaces, so using this feature can allow you to assign more detailed or more complete labels to your variables.

When importing your data to SPSS, you might start with demographic variables such as the participant's age and gender. These variables are important to note because they will need to be reported in the write-up of your methodology when you discuss your participant sample – you need to provide sufficient information for your study to be replicated, including details about how many males and females took part in the study, and what the age range and mean age of the sample was. Age is fairly simple as it is already in numerical form, although it may need to be converted to take account of months as well as years if neces-sary. Gender will usually have two potential categories, and you can identify these using the 'Values' feature (6th column in Variable View).

To assign a value to a variable, click on the relevant field within the value column and click the three dots on the right-hand side of the field. This will open a screen where you can allocate labels to different values – remember that you are conducting quantitative analysis so your variables will need to have numerical values – in the values box, you can assign, for example, a value of 1 to male and 2 to female. When you go back to the Data View page to enter your data, SPSS will then automatically recognise that every time you enter '1' in the gender column a participant is male, and every time you enter '2' in the gender column a participant is female. You can use the value feature in Variable View to assign values to any variable that has multiple categories. In doing so, you will be able to identify the levels of your independent variable(s). Before you can do this, of course, you need to be able to understand the different variables in your study – see our handy guide 'Understanding independent and dependent variables'.

Understanding independent and dependent variables

Independent variables

Independent variables are the variables that can be manipulated and have an effect on your outcome (dependent) variable(s). By 'manipulated' we mean that by changing the independent variable, you expect to see a different effect on the dependent variable. Independent variables will have multiple levels, which you might be trying to compare. For example, you might be looking at the differences between males and females on a particular outcome measure – in this case, gender will be the independent variable, with two levels: male and female. By changing the independent variable (i.e. by looking at female participants instead of male participants), you might expect to see a change in the dependent variable. Alternatively, you might be looking at the difference between two groups of participants on their performance on a particular task – in this case, the group would be your independent variable, and the number of groups you have would be the number of levels of the independent variable. Depending on the design of your study, you might have more than one independent variable. For example, you could be looking at the effects of multiple variables on an outcome measure, such as the effects of treatment group, gender and age group on participants' views of a particular phenomenon (where treatment group, gender and age group would all be independent variables). Importantly, in order to be used as an independent variable, you must be able to put participants' responses on each independent variable into categories (also called 'levels', such as 'male' and 'female', for example – the two levels of the 'gender' variable). It is also important to consider that your independent variable(s) can be either **between groups** (i.e. where participants are either in one group/category or the other, such as gender) or **within groups** (where participants are in multiple groups – e.g. if your participants complete all conditions within the study).

Dependent variables

Dependent variables are variables that can be measured (i.e. what you are studying), such as self-esteem or reading ability. Dependent variables can also be called outcome variables or outcome measures. They are usually measured on a continuous scale and are not intended to place participants into categories.

Importantly, the number of independent variables, the number of levels of the independent variable(s), whether your independent variable(s) are between or within groups variables, and the number of dependent variables you have within your study will all influence the type of statistical test that you can use to analyse your data. But it is not just the number of variables you have that will have an effect on the type of analysis you can run; we must also consider the *type* of variable(s) you have.

When we consider *type*, we are concerned with how the variables are measured (i.e. what scale is used). You can change the format of your variables using the 'Type' column (2nd column) in Variable View – it is important to do this because SPSS will not allow you to conduct certain methods of analysis if you do not have a suitable type of data. Before you can do this, you need to understand the different types of variables that exist, and what these different variable types mean.

Variable types

There are four main types of data collected in psychological research. As you move down the list, each type of data provides more information than the previous type: as such, ordinal data is also nominal; interval data is also ordinal and nominal; and ratio data is also interval, ordinal and nominal. The type of data you have will influence your options when it comes to data analysis, as some methods require the data to be of a specific type.

- **Nominal data**: Nominal data are named so because the word 'nominal' comes from the Latin *nomen*, meaning 'name'. Nominal data are classified by named categories, for example 'students', 'nationality' or 'group'. Nominal data do not provide any further information other than the name of the category, so what we can do with the data is limited.
- **Ordinal data**: Ordinal data allow us to place items into an order depending on their position on a given scale, for example 'position in a race', 'salary' or 'socio-economic status'. Importantly, ordinal data are sequential – we can place items in order within their nominal category, but the difference between each category on the scale is not defined, so the distance between the categories may vary greatly.

(Continued)

123

- **Interval data**: Interval data are more sophisticated and measure data along a more specific scale, where each item is an equal distance from the next. The use of interval data is common in psychological research where the researcher might be assessing participants on a scale between two extremes, for example using a Likert scale from 1 to 10, where responses are specified and participants can be rated or perform at any of the 10 points on the scale. Other examples of interval data are 'age in whole months', 'distance in feet' or 'temperature in degrees Celsius' (note that in all of these examples we are specifying the scale on which the category is measured, such that the distance between each point on the scale is equal).
- **Ratio data**: Ratio data are more sophisticated still. They allow us not only to place items in order on a given scale, but also allow us to compare items as multiples of one another – for example, recognising that one participant might be twice as quick as another participant when timed in seconds (remember that we need to specify the scale here because the data are more than ordinal). Both interval and ratio data allow us to measure quantities – hence, they are quantitative in nature, so they are suitable for many quantitative analysis methods. As both interval and ratio data are measured on a scale, they can also be referred to as *scale* data (remember this, as SPSS refers to *scale* data rather than 'interval' or 'ratio'!).

Once you have understood the variables in your study and the variable types, you will need to input this information to SPSS Variable View, to set up your spreadsheet ready for your data. If you are struggling, ask your supervisor to check and confirm that you have set up your Variable View correctly before you start inputting your data, but remember that your dissertation is intended to be an independent research project, so you will need to show that you have at least attempted to do this by yourself.

Next, you're ready to start inputting your data. Go to the 'Data View' tab at the bottom of your SPSS screen. You will see that your variable names now appear at the top of each column. Start inserting the data from each participant in a single row, completing their gender, age, group(s) and their scores for each variable. Repeat this process for each participant until all of your data have been inserted.

10.3 Screening and cleaning your data

Once you have entered your data into SPSS, the first thing to do is to check your data for outliers and ensure that you have entered all of the data correctly. This is an important step in preparing for data analysis and should not be overlooked, as any outliers or flaws in the data set could have an influence on the results from your analysis. Even the most competent researcher will make mistakes when entering data (we are only human, after all) – for example, entering a score of 1 or 100 instead of 10. You should scan your data manually, looking for any scores that stand out which could have been entered incorrectly. Double-checking these items against the original raw data can confirm whether a mistake has been made or whether there is a legitimate outlier. Outliers can be caused by various confounding factors. For example, a participant may have neglected to answer a particular question, resulting in a score of 0 (which may then be considered as a 'low' score, subsequently affecting the results). Other confounds include influences over participants' abilities to understand the questions, or to perform at the expected rate, such as special educational needs or disabilities which may not have been taken into account as exclusion criteria when designing the study. Where outliers are extreme and might have an effect on the results like this, they may need to be screened out (i.e. removed from the data set). However, this should only be done if you have a legitimate reason to believe that the participant either didn't complete the study as intended, or that the participant doesn't belong to the population you intended to test. If you do screen out participants from the data set, it is important to note that this will reduce the size of your sample, so you will also need to alter the participant details reported in your methodology accordingly. You will be able to read more about outliers in specialist research methods textbooks such as those recommended at earlier stages in your course, or by revisiting course content.

Another thing to consider when cleaning your data is whether you have all of the variables you need in the data set in order to be able to answer your research question(s) sufficiently. For example, if you have used a questionnaire with 20 different items, are you interested in the scores for each individual item, or the total score, or both, or scores for groups of items? You will need to consider whether you have created columns for each of these 'variables', or whether you need to create additional variables (e.g. to create a 'Total Score' column) – you can do this using the 'compute variable' feature in SPSS if needed.

10.4 Descriptive statistics

Once you have screened your data and ensured that they are clean and ready for analysis, you are ready to begin analysing. The first things you will need to report in your results section are the descriptive statistics, including the means and standard deviations of the data relevant to each of your variables.

Some definitions

- **Descriptive statistics**: A summary of the distributions of the data, including consideration of averages, ranges and dispersion.
- **Central tendency**: A scientific way of referring to the 'middle' or 'centre' of a distribution, for example by measuring the mean, median or mode.
- **Mean**: The mathematical average of a data set – calculated by adding together all of the values in a list and dividing the total by the number of items. You can only calculate the mean of interval or ratio data ('scale' data); you cannot apply this calculation to ordinal or nominal data (because data needs to be quantified in numbers in order to mathematically calculate something).
- **Median**: The midpoint of a list of data – calculated by arranging all items in order (usually in ascending order) and identifying the value in the middle of the list. The median is a useful calculation to use for ordinal data, as it allows us to identify the midpoint without being concerned about the extremity of values at either end of the scale. For example, if the person at the top of the list had an extreme height of 7ft 5, this would push the mean participant height up (compared to the person at the top of the list having a height of 6ft 6, for example), but this would not affect the median. However, as the median overlooks extreme values, it can give an inaccurate representation of the average of the data, so calculating the mean would be more accurate, if possible.
- **Mode**: The most common value within a data set, calculated by looking at the number of participants in each category of data – for example, are there more participants that fall under the category of 'teenager', 'young adult' or 'older adult'? The most common response would be the mode, which is a useful measure of central tendency for nominal data, as this type of data is reliant on categories so it cannot be subject to mathematical calculation.
- **Dispersion**: A measurement of the spread of the data. Dispersion can be measured by looking at the range, variance or standard deviation of a data set.
- **Range**: The most straightforward way of measuring dispersion, calculated by subtracting the lowest value from the highest value in the data set. For example, if participants varied in age from 18 years to 38 years, the range would be 20 years. Importantly, we should consider the limitation of using the range as a measure of dispersion. With range, we have the opposite issue to that which we encounter when we look at the median: where median does not take into account extreme values, the range focuses solely on these extreme values at either end of the scale and does not consider the values in between.
- **Inter-quartile range**: A measure of dispersion focusing on the 'middle 50 per cent' of the data. This calculation involves splitting your data into four equal quartiles and focusing only on the middle 50 per cent (ignoring the top 25% and the bottom 25%) to give an indication of where the majority of the data lie. This is a useful measure of spread for data where the central tendency is measured by the median, as it similarly requires data to be 'in order'.

- **Variance and standard deviation**: The variance of a data set refers to the spread of data around the mean and is generally considered a good measure of dispersion. Variance is calculated by working out the average of the squared differences from the mean – this is only possible for interval or ratio data, where you can calculate a mean in the first place. Standard deviation is the square root of the variance and is the most commonly reported calculation of dispersion.

10.4.1 Reporting descriptive statistics

Quantitative research requires that you report both the descriptive statistics (including some indication of the central tendency and dispersion of the data) and the inferential statistics (results from your main analysis). We will talk more about inferential statistics later, but first let's consider the descriptive statistics. The measure of central tendency in your report will depend on the type of data you have (see our guide above in section 10.4 for understanding different measures). However, the most common way of reporting central tendency is through the mean, with standard deviation reported as a measure of dispersion. The means and standard deviations for your data set can be reported either in the text or a table (not both – avoid repetition). Some examples are provided in Figure 10.3.

In female participants ($N = 49$), the mean word reading score was 107.94 (s.d. = 12.41), the mean comprehension score was 94.37 (s.d. = 10.74) and the mean fluency score was 10.41 (s.d. = 4.62). In male participants ($N = 33$), the mean word reading score was 104.32 (s.d. = 11.29), the mean comprehension score was 92.14 (s.d. = 7.88) and the mean fluency score was 9.57 (s.d. = 3.91).

OR

Table 1

Table of means and standard deviations

Variable	Gender	Mean	SD
Word reading	Female	107.94	12.41
	Male	104.32	11.29
Comprehension	Female	94.37	10.74
	Male	92.14	7.88
Fluency	Female	10.41	4.62
	Male	9.57	3.91

Note that both the mean and standard deviation in each case are reported to two decimal places.

Figure 10.3   Example of reporting descriptive statistics in the text and in a table

10.5 Parametric assumptions

Whilst the descriptive statistics provide us with some indication of the average scores on each variable and the spread of the data, they do not help us to identify whether there are significant differences between groups or significant relationships between variables, which you might need to establish in order to answer your research question(s). To address this, you will need to conduct your main analysis, but before you can do so, you need to determine whether your data meet parametric assumptions and therefore whether a parametric test is appropriate.

What do we mean by 'parametric assumptions', and why are they important?

Parametric assumptions are the assumptions that a parametric test makes about the data you are analysing. You need to make sure that your data meet parametric assumptions before you conduct a parametric test because any violation of these assumptions can affect the accuracy of the results. You will need to demonstrate that you have checked to ensure your data meet parametric assumptions before conducting your main analysis.

The first main assumption of parametric testing is that the data are measured on an interval or ratio scale – see our explanations in section 10.2 about different types of data. In order to conduct a parametric test, you must have either interval or ratio level data, because data need to be quantified to this level in order to run mathematical analyses. You must also ensure that participants are a random sample from a defined population – this should be considered within your project planning.

10.5.1 Normality

The second main assumption of parametric testing is the assumption of normality. This means that your data are normally distributed – that is, that they form a bell-shaped curve when presented in a graph (Figure 10.4). If your data are normally distributed, the data will be symmetrical, with the mean, median and mode all coinciding at the highest point of the curve.

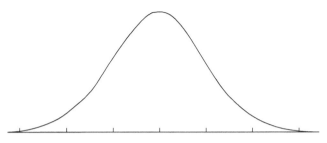

Figure 10.4　Normal distribution/bell-curve image

If the data are not symmetrical (such as in Figure 10.5), the distribution can be considered as either positively skewed (where the highest point of the curve appears at the lower end of the distribution, with the tail pointing towards the higher or more positive scores) or negatively skewed (where the highest point of the curve appears at the higher end of the distribution, with the tail pointing towards the lower or more negative scores).

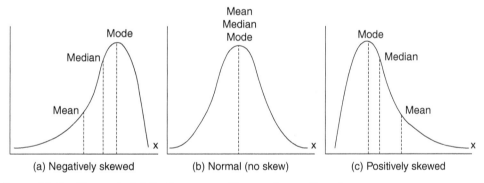

Figure 10.5　Skewed distributions – positive and negative skew

---

Skew: A measure of the symmetry of a distribution. Symmetrical (normal) distributions will have a skew of 0.

A normal distribution will have a skew value of 0, so any deviation from 0 indicates that the data are skewed in some way. The further the skew value is from zero, the more skewed the data are, and the higher the probability that the assumption of normality may have been violated. It is commonly accepted that a skew value of between -2 and +2 is acceptable, but anything beyond this, in either direction, is likely to violate the assumption of normality. In order to be certain that your data are not overly skewed, you can calculate the z-score of the skewness. To do this, start with the skew value, subtract the mean of the distribution and then divide the total by the standard deviation of the distribution (standard error). The resulting z-score should then be compared to what we might expect to achieve by chance – so a z-score of more than 1.96 would be significant at $p<.05$, a z-score of above 2.58 would be significant at $p<.01$ and a z-score of above 3.29 would be significant at $p<.001$.

When we consider the assumption of normality, we are also concerned with kurtosis. This is another measure of the spread of data within the distribution. Normal distributions will have a kurtosis value of 0. A distribution with positive kurtosis (i.e. a score of more than 0) is one where a lot of scores are present in the 'tails', such that the distribution is tall and thin. This is known as a **leptokurtic** distribution. A distribution with negative kurtosis (i.e. a score of less than 0) is one where there are very few scores in the 'tails', such that the distribution is wide and flat. This is known as a **platykurtic** distribution (see Figure 10.6).

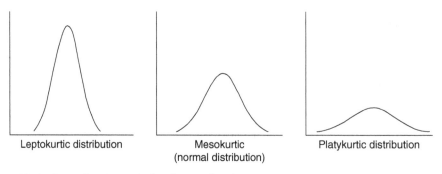

| Leptokurtic distribution | Mesokurtic (normal distribution) | Platykurtic distribution |

Figure 10.6 Leptokurtic and platykurtic distributions

Kurtosis: A measure of the degree to which scores are clustered in the 'tails' of a distribution. A normal distribution will have a kurtosis value of 0.

As with skew, you can calculate the z-score of the kurtosis of your data by starting with the kurtosis value, subtracting the mean of the distribution and dividing the total by the standard deviation of the distribution (standard error). The resulting z-score should then be compared to what we might expect to achieve by chance (see our discussion above about z-scores).

Skew and kurtosis in large samples

Be wary of using significance tests of skew and kurtosis in studies with large samples – when your sample size is large, it is likely that skew and kurtosis z-scores will be significant, even when the skew and kurtosis values are not too far from normal.

The most commonly used tests of normality in SPSS are the Shapiro-Wilk's W test (widely applicable) and the Kolmogorov-Smirnov test (used more for large samples). In both of these tests, the result should *not* be significant (i.e. $p > .05$) in order to meet the assumption of normality, because a result on these tests that is not significant essentially tells us that the distribution is *not significantly different from a normal distribution*. You can read more about these tests in more specialist research methods textbooks such as those recommended for your research methods modules.

Writing about parametric assumptions in your results chapter: Normality

When you write up your results chapter, you will need to demonstrate that you have checked your data for parametric assumptions prior to conducting your main analysis. The first thing to report is that the data have been checked for normality of variance, and that there are no issues with skew and kurtosis. Or, if there are any issues, you will need to explain how you have overcome them to ensure that the assumption of normality has been met (we will discuss transforming your data later on), or what you have done instead (i.e. conducted a non-parametric test – again, we will discuss this later). You may be expected to include a histogram to visually represent the distribution of your data and/or to report values of skew and kurtosis. In your dissertation, it will usually be acceptable to evidence these calculations and checks in an appendix, but check with your supervisor whether they would prefer you to include this information in the main results chapter (remember, they will be marking your work).

10.5.2 Homogeneity of variance

The third assumption of parametric testing is homogeneity of variance – that is, the assumption that the variance of one variable is stable across all levels of another variable. Essentially, this means that, as one variable changes, you should not see a change in the variance of another variable.

There are two different ways of looking at homogeneity of variance, and the use of these methods depends on the type of data you have collected and the type of analysis you plan to conduct. If you are conducting a study with continuous data, such as a correlation study, homogeneity of variance refers to the idea that as one variable changes, you should not see a change in the variance of your other variable. You can assess homogeneity of variance for a correlation analysis or regression analysis by looking at the scatter plots to gain a visual representation of the variance of the data.

Alternatively, if you are conducting a study looking at different groups of participants, the variance of your outcome variable (dependent variable) should be the same in each group. You can test homogeneity of variance between groups using Levene's test (Levene, 1960). SPSS will conduct this for you, but let us explain this step by step for your understanding:

- We want to test the null hypothesis that the variances of your groups are all equal – that is, that the difference between the variances is 0 (H_1 is therefore 'there is a significant difference between the variances of your groups').
- Levene's test assesses whether the differences between the variances of your groups is significant (therefore testing the hypotheses above).
- If Levene's test is significant (i.e. if $p<.05$) then we can conclude that the difference between the variances is significant. H_1 can therefore be accepted and the null hypothesis can be rejected. If this is the case, then the assumption of homogeneity of variance has been violated, because we want the variances to be equal (i.e. no significant difference between the variances of your groups).
- If Levene's test is not significant (i.e. if $p \geq .05$) then we can conclude that there are no significant differences between the variances of your groups, so the assumption of homogeneity of variance has not been violated (i.e. the assumption has been met).

Writing about parametric assumptions in your results chapter: Homogeneity of variance

When you discuss checks for parametric assumptions within your results chapter, you should report the result of Levene's test to show that you have considered the assumption of homogeneity of variance. The result of Levene's test should be reported using an F-statistic and be written as: $F(df1, df2)$ = Levene's value, p = sig value.

10.5.3 Multicollinearity

The fourth assumption of parametric testing refers to multicollinearity, or rather, the assumption that there is no multicollinearity between variables. Multicollinearity means that there are high correlations between the variables in the study, which should not be the case if your variables are adding value to your analysis (i.e. all of your variables should measure something different). This assumption is especially important if you are conducting a regression analysis, as we would expect that each of the predictor variables would explain a certain proportion of unique variance in the outcome variable.

To test the assumption of multicollinearity, you should check three things:

1. The Pearson correlation table should show that none of the variables are highly correlated with another (all correlations should be below .8).
2. The tolerance values for all variables should be above .1, since the variables tolerance is 1-R2, so a small tolerance value (i.e. below .1) indicates that the variable is almost a perfect linear combination of the independent variables already in the equation.
3. The variance inflation factor (VIF) values for all variables should be below 10. The VIF measures the impact of collinearity on the variables in the model. Since the VIF is equivalent to 1/tolerance, the VIF is always greater than or equal to 1, but there is no definitive value for VIF which determines that multicollinearity, although values that exceed 10 may indicate that there may be an issue.

Writing about parametric assumptions in your results chapter: Multicollinearity

When you discuss multicollinearity within your results chapter, you should report the result of these checks: report that none of the variables are highly correlated (that all are below .8), that the tolerance values are all above .1 and that VIF values are all below 10.

10.5.4 What to do if your data violate assumptions for parametric testing

If your data do not meet the assumptions for parametric testing, you have two different options: either you transform your data so that they do meet parametric assumptions, or you conduct a non-parametric equivalent of the analysis you had intended to conduct. Before you do either though, it is important to check the data for outliers. In section 10.3, we discussed the importance of checking your data for any mistakes that could have occurred during the data-input stage. If you skipped that part, it is worth checking now whether there are any outliers in the data, and whether they could be the result of human error when entering your data into SPSS. If outliers remain after you have checked for errors, it is important to consider why you might have obtained any extreme cases (refer back to our discussion in section 10.3), and whether these cases need to be removed. If you don't have a legitimate reason for removing any outliers, then it is important to consider that these outliers may cause a skewed distribution, meaning that the assumption of normality may be violated. Your next option is to transform the data to see if this reduces the skewness and brings your data closer to meeting parametric assumptions.

You can transform your data in many different ways using SPSS. Here are the main options:

- Log transformation ($\log(X_i)$)
- Square root transformation ($\sqrt{X_i}$)
- Reciprocal transformation ($1/X_i$)
- Reverse score transformation.

Log transformations, square root transformations and reciprocal transformations can all help to correct for positive skew or unequal variances in the data, but they are relevant in different situations (depending on the characteristics of your data). By reversing the scores of any of these first three types of transformation, you can use reverse score transformation to help to correct for negative skew. As we mentioned earlier, we'd advise you to check more specialised research methods texts for further information on these specific types of transformations.

Initially, it can be difficult to identify which transformation you should use. There is no right or wrong answer regarding which transformation is best – as already mentioned, this largely depends on the characteristics of your data. Our advice would be to use trial and error – if a particular transformation doesn't have any effect on the results of your tests for parametric assumptions, try another transformation instead. Importantly, if your study is concerned with comparing variables, you must apply the same transformation to *all* of your variables (you can't use one transformation on one variable and another transformation on a different variable).

You can learn more about transforming your data in specialist research methods textbooks or by using the advanced content of your course (emphasis on 'advanced' – many undergraduate courses don't cover transformation of data, so check your course content first. If transformation isn't covered on your course, this doesn't mean you can't do it – instead, you have an opportunity to demonstrate what you can learn and conduct independently).

10.5.5 Non-parametric testing

If you have exhausted your transformation options and there is still no effect on the results of your test(s) of parametric assumptions, then you may need to conduct a non-parametric equivalent analysis.

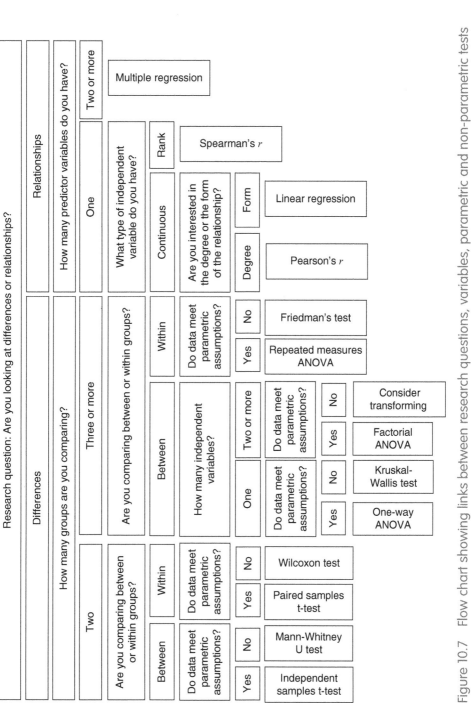

Figure 10.7   Flow chart showing links between research questions, variables, parametric and non-parametric tests

Use the information you identified earlier (variables, types, etc.), along with the knowledge of whether your data meet parametric assumptions or not, to help you to identify the data analysis method you should use to help you answer your research question. See Figure 10.7 to help you determine which data analysis technique is most suitable for your data.

10.6 Inferential statistics

After you have reported the descriptive statistics in your dissertation and explained that you have screened the data for parametric assumptions, the next thing you will report will be the inferential statistics (your main analysis). Before you report the results of the main analysis, you will need to justify why the test you have chosen is an appropriate method of data analysis for your study (remember what we discussed earlier – the key to producing a strong argument and narrative throughout your dissertation is to clearly justify all of the decisions you make). It would be impossible for us to go into detail about every possible method of data analysis here, so you should consult more specialised research methods textbooks for further details on how to conduct and report the results of individual analytic techniques.

10.7 Statistical significance

Many research questions and analysis methods will be centred on establishing statistical significance in your results. Statistical significance is the probability of rejecting the null hypothesis, given that the null hypothesis is assumed to be true. To calculate statistical significance, you must first define the probability of a sampling error. A sampling error exists to some extent within any study that does not test the entire population (the vast majority of studies, then, since it would be almost impossible to test an entire population, especially if your study is based on a large generic population such as students or nurses). It is important to make sure that when working with a sample from a given population, the sample is representative of the population they are selected from. Any error in the sampling technique can lead to an unrepresentative sample, and, as such, your data may not provide an accurate representation of what we might expect to find in the whole population. This is known as the sampling error. The error rate is denoted by alpha (α) and is 5 per cent in most psychological research. This means that we have a 5 per cent chance of a sampling error, or of finding something in the general population that is not represented in our sample of participants. Generally, the larger the sample size, the less probability of a sampling error, because we would expect a larger sample to be more representative of the population.

As researchers, we refer to statistical significance through the use of a p-value, and in order for the findings of the analysis to be significant, p must be below .05. If, as discussed, $p<.05$, this indicates that there is a significant probability that the results did *not* occur by chance, and so we can reject the null hypothesis. It is imperative that you are able to understand (and demonstrate your understanding of) significance testing and reporting in your results chapter, so make the most of supervision and formative opportunities.

Common mistakes when reporting findings

- Not understanding '<' (less than) and '>' (more than)
- Not understanding, or misreporting, decimal places – make sure you understand the difference between .5 and .05, for example
- Not using APA formatting – remember to use italics where relevant, and understand how to present tables and figures
- Not understanding the findings of the data analysis – take the time to read about your analytic method(s) in detail and ensure that you fully understand what analysis you have conducted and what the results mean
- Neglecting to include a clear, thorough narrative throughout the results chapter.

Chapter summary

In this chapter, we have discussed the steps in preparing for data analysis, different types of variable and data, parametric assumptions and details of writing up your results chapter. You should use the information to help you to prepare and analyse your data and write up your results chapter. It is important to use the information alongside more specialist research methods textbooks and guidance on data analysis and interpretation for specific analytic techniques. We would advise you to keep in regular contact with your supervisor during this process, and to make the most of any formative opportunities that your institution or department offers.

Homework

- Use the information in this chapter to help you to identify the most appropriate data analysis technique for your study.
- Attempt to conduct and write up your data analysis chapter.

Checklist

✓ Identify the data analysis technique you will use to analyse your data.

✓ Attempt your data analysis.

✓ Draft your data analysis chapter.

✓ Discuss your data analysis output/draft results with your supervisor.

✓ Start to think about how you might explain your results when it comes to the discussion chapter (this will be discussed in more detail in Chapter 13).

11

Qualitative Data Analysis

As discussed earlier, qualitative research involves the collection of data in word form. This allows the researcher to seek in-depth, rich, meaningful data from participants that provide a detailed insight into their experiences, beliefs or attitudes. Common qualitative methodology involves the use of interviews or focus groups, or qualitative surveys where participants are presented with free text boxes to freely write their answers to the questions. If you are conducting a qualitative research project for your dissertation, you will likely need to transcribe these data obtained through your qualitative methodology (particularly if you have conducted interviews or focus groups). This chapter will provide a guide to the transcription and analysis of qualitative data.

Learning outcomes

By the end of this chapter you will:

- Understand the different types of transcription for qualitative data and how to identify the most appropriate method for your study
- Understand the differences and similarities between types of qualitative analysis
- Understand the processes of generating codes and generating themes from these codes
- Understand the basics of reporting qualitative research findings.

11.1 Transcription

The first step in qualitative research is to transcribe your data. Transcription is relevant where you have conducted interviews or focus groups with participants and have recorded them using a recording device. The spoken language will need to be converted into written text in order to prepare for analysis. If you have conducted surveys (i.e. where the data are already in written form), transcription won't be necessary. Although transcription is the initial process in preparing for data analysis, it involves some analytical thinking, allowing the researcher to familiarise themselves with the data and to start thinking about how they might begin to interpret what the participants have said. As such, transcription itself can be considered the first stage of data analysis.

11.1.1 Types of transcription

Before you can begin to transcribe your data, you will need to identify the most appropriate method of transcription for your study. This will largely depend on what it is that you are investigating, what your research question is and how you are planning to analyse your data, as different types of analysis will require different forms of transcription.

Transcription can be categorised as being either orthographic or playscript, or non-orthographic. Orthographic transcription requires the researcher to write down everything the participant has said, word for word, exactly as they have said it. This is known as a verbatim representation of the participants' spoken accounts, and, as such, this method is widely known as the verbatim method of transcription. Verbatim (i.e. orthographic) transcription is most suitable if you are mainly concerned with *what* participants have said (as opposed to *how* they have said it). This would be most relevant to analytic methods such as thematic analysis, interpretative phenomenological analysis (IPA) or grounded theory, which involve finding themes in the content of the data.

In comparison, the non-orthographic or Jeffersonian (named after its creator Gail Jefferson) method of transcription focuses not just on what was said, but also on *how* participants used language to convey meaning. This method captures additional paralinguistic features of the language participants have used, such as pauses, pitch, intonation, emphasis and volume. Where the researcher has access to non-linguistic features of the interaction, such as when the data have been captured via video recording, Jeffersonian transcription also allows the researcher to take note of extralinguistic features such as body language and non-verbal behaviours which may also convey meaning. Jeffersonian transcription would be most suitable for analytic methods such as discourse analysis, which is concerned with what participants are *doing* with their language.

It is important that you are able to demonstrate to your examiners that you understand the relevance of the transcription method you have chosen, not only to the analytic method that follows, but also to your theoretical perspective (which should be clear in your literature review), your research question(s) and your methodology. Think about what you want to find out from your participants – if your research question is simply about *what* participants report, verbatim transcription should provide you with a detailed-enough account of the interaction. However, if you are concerned with participants' body language or *how* they report their experiences or attitudes, Jeffersonian transcription would provide you with more information about the ways in which the participants have interacted during the data collection phase.

Transcription tips

- Be aware of the time needed for transcription. On average, it takes around one hour for every ten minutes of recording – so, if you have ten 30-minute interviews to transcribe, you can expect this to take you approximately 30 hours. It would be wise to plan ahead, taking this timescale into consideration.
- Use a recording device with the 'slow down' facility. This will enable you to slow down playback during transcription to a speed that corresponds to your typing ability.

11.2 Types of qualitative analysis: Which one is most suitable for your research?

In this section, we will discuss the different types of qualitative analysis, describing each method so that you can identify which one is most suitable for your project. It would be advisable to discuss this with your supervisor so that you can ensure that they are happy with the approach you have chosen to take – remember, they will be marking your work, so it needs to be clear to them that you understand why this approach is the most suitable and why/how it will help you to answer your research question(s). Ideally, you should have a good idea of the type of analysis you will run when you design your study because, as already discussed, you need to ensure that there is a clear narrative running through your dissertation, showing how each section of your work maps on to the next – as such, there should be a clear link between the research discussed in your literature review, your own research question(s), your chosen methodology (and the questions included in your interview/focus group/survey) and your chosen method of data analysis. However, in real-world research we understand that sometimes our research questions might change slightly during the course of the project, so here we will discuss when each method of analysis would be most suitable and for which types of project/question. As we discuss each method of analysis, you will notice that there are lots of similarities, and only subtle differences, between the different approaches, so your choice of analysis needs to be justified clearly in the write-up of your dissertation to build a strong case for why it is the most appropriate method to use. Our advice would be to read as widely as you can around your chosen method to ensure that you have a thorough understanding of the background of the approach and the processes involved. There are many textbooks that we could recommend on qualitative research skills and analysis, but it would be advisable to consult the core texts for your course, perhaps starting with those from your research methods module(s) earlier in your course.

So which approach should you choose? Our flowchart in Figure 11.1 shows when certain approaches may be appropriate.

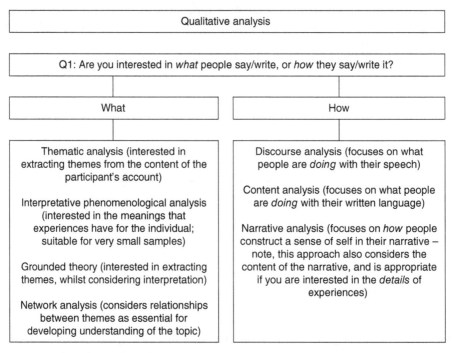

Figure 11.1 Flowchart of qualitative analysis approaches

Qualitative methods of data analysis can be split into two categories: those that are driven by theory and those that are driven by the data. Theory-driven approaches are useful when you want to apply specific theoretical concepts to the study data, that is, to assess whether or not these concepts can be applied to the data and therefore whether the theory can explain the data you have collected. Data-driven approaches, on the other hand, are more open-minded, and aim to be independent of theoretical concepts. In conducting a data-driven qualitative analysis, one must try to avoid starting with any pre-determined theoretical concepts, ideas, or predictions about the data. This forms a challenge for researchers, because, as our knowledge about a subject grows, it becomes increasingly difficult to ignore all of our preconceptions. For this reason, many qualitative approaches include an element of reflexivity, allowing the researcher to reflect on how these preconceived ideas and concepts might influence how we design and conduct the study, and how they might influence the themes we generate from the data.

11.2.1 Thematic analysis

Thematic analysis is perhaps the most widely used method of qualitative analysis. This may be due to its flexibility, which means that it is not bound to any specific theoretical approach. Indeed, Braun and Clarke (2006) argued that thematic analysis is the foundation for qualitative analysis, as a number of the principles are relevant to many other approaches (some of which we will discuss later). In particular, we should pay attention to the principle of 'coding', which underpins methods such as interpretative phenomenological analysis (IPA) and grounded theory. However, despite the overlap with other approaches to data analysis, Braun and Clarke also argued that thematic analysis should be considered as a method in its own right. In contrast to approaches such as discourse analysis, which takes into consideration the *way* people say things (we will discuss this more later), thematic analysis is mainly concerned with the generation of themes from the *content* of participants' accounts.

What is a theme?

According to Braun and Clarke (2006, p. 82), a theme 'captures something important about the data in relation to the research question, and represents some level of patterned response or *meaning* within the data set'. Essentially, themes represent *meaning* within the data – they identify categories within participants' responses. These categories may form the theme names, and multiple smaller themes may be grouped together as subthemes of a main theme. The number of themes one generates from a data set is flexible and depends on many aspects of the research such as the research question(s), methodology and the variance within and between participants' responses.

Braun and Clarke (2006) identified six steps to conducting thematic analysis:

1. **Familiarisation with the data**: The researcher immerses themselves in the data to the extent that they are familiar with the depth and breadth of the content.

2. **Generating initial codes**: The researcher begins to identify meaningful features of the data. This might involve making notes as you read the data, annotating and/or high-lighting the transcripts to identify interesting points or features.
3. **Searching for themes**: The researcher re-focuses their attention on the broader themes that might result from groups or categories of codes. Codes may be given names and may become themes or subthemes in the final report.
4. **Reviewing themes**: This involves reviewing and refining the initial list of themes, removing or combining any with insufficient data to support them, or breaking larger themes into smaller separate themes. By the time this stage is complete, you should have a rough list of themes for the final report, and an understanding of how they all relate to one another and contribute to our understanding of the topic.
5. **Defining and naming themes**: This involves further refinement, and consideration of how each theme fits into the story you are trying to tell in your report.
6. **Writing the report – the final stage**: This requires the researcher to produce a coherent, logical and interesting account of the story the data tell.

Essential reading: Thematic analysis

Braun, V. and Clarke, V. (2006) Using thematic analysis in psychology. *Qualitative Research in Psychology*, 3(2), 77–101.

11.2.2 Interpretative phenomenological analysis (IPA)

Interpretative phenomenological analysis (IPA) is interested in the individual experiences of the participants and the meanings that these experiences have for the individuals. The aim of IPA is to achieve a deep and rich account of the experience of each individual participant, such that the researcher is able to gain a deep and meaningful insight into individual cases. This is in contrast to other methods of analysis that might make generalisable claims or conclusions about the findings, such as what you might do when conducting a study with a large-scale survey. IPA would be an appropriate choice of analysis if you were planning to work with a very small sample size, or if you wanted to gain an insight into individual case studies, having conducted, for example, semi-structured interviews on a one-to-one basis with your participants.

Like other methods of qualitative analysis such as thematic analysis, IPA involves an initial stage of coding the data, making notes on anything of interest or that might be relevant to the formation of themes later in the analysis. However, unlike other methods of analysis, IPA also takes a unique perspective on phenomenology and interpretation. IPA considers interpretation on two levels – it considers firstly that the participant has had to interpret their experience themselves, so what the researcher receives in the form of data for the study is not necessarily a true picture of the event in question; instead, it is the participant's account of that experience, subject to their own interpretation. As a result, the researcher then has to interpret the participant's interpretation of their experiences. This two-sided approach to interpretation is known as the double hermeneutic.

Importantly, this double hermeneutic takes into consideration the active role of the researcher in the interpretation of the participant's experiences. It considers, for example, how the researcher's prior knowledge or own experiences might influence how they interpret the data from the participant(s). As such, IPA also emphasises the importance of reflexivity – that is, reflection about how you as a researcher have interpreted the data. Importantly, this reflection is relevant to your own (i.e. individual) interpretation, and it is important to consider that another researcher analysing the same data may have a very different interpretation from yours. If you are conducting IPA in your research, it would be useful to keep a reflective diary during the process of data analysis to record your thoughts, impressions and interpretations of the data.

11.2.3 Grounded theory

Grounded theory (Glaser & Strauss, 1967) describes the process of drawing themes from qualitative data, taking interpretation into consideration. In the process of generating themes from the data, we develop a theoretical stand-point in relation to the data – in this way, we do not start with a theory, but rather arrive at a theory as a result of the analysis (i.e. the theory is grounded in the data, hence the name 'grounded theory'), so the process is very much data driven (see our earlier discussion of data-driven versus theory-driven analyses).

Grounded theory focuses on the development of themes from the data in a series of stages, and, like network analysis (which will be discussed later), grounded theory also considers how themes may be related to one another. Grounded theorists such as Strauss and Corbin (1990) have provided names for each stage of the coding process:

1. **Open coding**: This is the initial stage, whereby you examine the data in detail, compar-ing each part of the data to the rest, and so on, so that you can place data into categories. This is where you might go through the data using different coloured highlighters, identifying similar data in the same colour. You might have just a handful of open codes or many more. The number of open codes largely depends on your data, so it would be wrong for us to put a number on it here.
2. **Axial coding**: Here you begin to interpret what the open codes might mean. In this stage it is typical for the researcher to begin to identify appropriate names or labels for the open codes identified in stage 1.

3. **Selective coding**: This is where the main themes are identified – 'the process of selecting the core category' as Strauss and Corbin (1990, p. 116) described it, whereby the researcher thinks systematically about the relationships between variables, and where themes are refined and developed further.

Throughout these stages, you will likely be making notes about potential themes in the data, and associations between them, a process which Strauss and Corbin called 'memoing'. This process is very similar to the notes you might make during the process of conducting IPA (you would note your thoughts, ideas and reflections on the data). So, you can see how the different types of analysis are similar to one another.

11.2.4 Network analysis

Network analysis is similar to grounded theory in that it allows the researcher to consider how the resulting themes may be related to one another but considers these relationships as being central to its methodology. In writing up the findings of a network analysis, the researcher would aim to explain how these themes

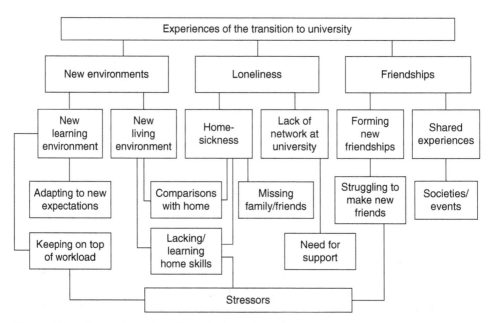

Figure 11.2   Example network analysis map

Note: This is an *example* of how a network analysis map might be formed; your network map might differ in style, depending on the number of themes and subthemes you extract from the data and how they link together.

might 'map on' to one another using 'networks' which act and look like (when we draw a diagram) branches of a tree. In this way, each theme leads to multiple subthemes. This is particularly useful if you have lots of subthemes within a main theme, and if those subthemes might comprise of lots of different codes within the data. By creating this 'map' of themes and subthemes, network analysis allows the researcher to organise or arrange these themes and sub-themes into hierarchical levels, whereby the reader can observe how higher order themes lead to subthemes, and so on. This is illustrated in Figure 11.2.

11.2.5 Narrative analysis

Narrative analysis focuses on how people construct a sense of self through an extensive narrative account of their life or of a particular experience. It is an in-depth analysis of multiple features of the narrative a participant has provided. Typically, narrative analysis would be an appropriate analytical method to use when you have an interest in the details of participants' lived experiences. It would follow on well from the use of semi-structured interviews, which allow the participant(s) to freely create a narrative about their life or a specific experience.

In the process of conducting narrative analysis, the researcher is interested in both the content *and* the form of the narrative. Depending on your research question(s), you might focus on the tone (i.e. is it optimistic or pessimistic?), the terminology (including the use of metaphors, similes, etc.) and the possible hidden messages (i.e. what the participant might mean by the narrative). With this last point, your interpretation of the data will be important – note the similarities here with other types of analysis that take interpretation into consideration.

11.2.6 Discourse analysis and content analysis

Discourse analysis is the study of language in social context – it is about what people are 'doing' with their language, or what they are trying to achieve with their speech. In discourse analysis, we are interested in the *words* that people choose to use and *how* they use them. By *how*, we are interested in the way they say things – focusing on features like emphasis, intonation and volume. If you are interested in the way people say things, discourse analysis will enable you to take this into consideration in your analysis, but you will need to ensure that you transcribe your data appropriately. This will include taking note of pauses (and their length), emphasis, tonal patterns and vowel lengths. Taking note of these features of the communication will allow you to consider what these features mean. For this reason, Jeffersonian transcription might be most appropriate, as it will provide you with a more accurate representation of the way in which your participants have spoken during the data collection process, but do discuss this with your supervisor first.

Like discourse analysis, content analysis also considers the role of language but is used when analysing written rather than spoken language – for example, when analysing data from surveys or questionnaires, where participants have been asked to write their answers down rather than speaking them out loud, as they would in an interview.

11.3 Reflexivity

Many of the analytic approaches above include some element of reflexivity. Being able to reflect on your influence over the data as a researcher is an important part of the process of qualitative research, not only because of your interpretation of the data, but also because you (as the researcher) have played a significant role in all stages of the research, from the writing of the research question, to the design of the study, the design of the questions that participants answer, the transcription of the data, the analysis and the construction of themes. Your existing knowledge and (probably subconscious) theoretical perspective of the topic will naturally have played a role in the decisions you have made throughout these processes, influencing bias and interpretation. Consideration of the role you have played in shaping the research is called reflexivity and is fundamental to successful qualitative research.

One of the ways in which you can include reflexivity in your project is to keep a reflective diary throughout the data analysis, noting your ideas, interpretations and opinions about the data. Keeping this reflective diary will allow you to look back reflectively on the process of analysis and to consider how your preconceptions might have influenced the themes that emerged from the data. In the write-up of a qualitative report, many researchers include a specific section on reflexivity, but ideally the reflexive element of qualitative analysis will be notable throughout the report.

11.4 Writing up your qualitative results chapter

The write-up of qualitative findings is fairly flexible and largely depends on personal preference as well as the type of analysis you have conducted. It goes without saying that you will need to report the findings of your analysis, explaining each of the resulting themes in detail with reference to the data (using quotes, where relevant, to link back to the transcripts). Many qualitative researchers combine the results and discussion chapters when writing up their research, but it would be advisable to discuss different approaches with your supervisor to get their opinion on what is most appropriate for your project. If you do combine your results and discussion chapters, you will need to discuss your findings in relation to previous research, your research question(s) and your theoretical perspective in a way that is similar to what you would do in the discussion chapter of a quantitative project. Within the description of findings, you'd also be expected to discuss any limitations of your methodology, and directions for future research. We will discuss how to write an effective discussion section in Chapter 13, and you should pay attention to this chapter regardless of whether you are doing quantitative or qualitative research, as the general expectations will be the same for all projects.

Chapter summary

In this chapter we have covered:

- Types of transcription and which methods are most appropriate to different analytic techniques
- Various methods of qualitative analysis, including details on their similarities and unique differences
- Details on how to begin thinking about writing up the results of a qualitative study.

You should now be prepared to begin transcribing and analysing your data. If you have any questions along the way, you can read more on qualitative research methods in the core texts for your course (namely your research methods module(s)). Your supervisor will also be able to provide further guidance.

Homework

Use the information in this chapter to help you to identify the most appropriate type of qualitative analysis to help you answer your research question. Attempt your data analysis and start to identify themes, and then book an appointment with your supervisor to discuss the resulting themes from your data analysis.

Checklist

✓ Identify and conduct your data analysis.

✓ Start to identify emerging themes in your data.

✓ Book an appointment with your supervisor to discuss your findings.

WRITING UP

This part of the book focuses on writing up your dissertation. Chapter 12 largely focuses on the writing skills that you will need to employ and demonstrate in the whole of your dissertation, and you should pay attention to this chapter throughout your dissertation module, not just when it comes to the writing-up stage. Many sections of your dissertation will start developing from early on in the module, or even before the module begins, so attending to principles of good writing style from the beginning will provide you with the foundations necessary for producing a well-structured and well-written dissertation.

The final chapter of your dissertation is the discussion, and this is likely to be the only chapter for which you do not have the opportunity to receive formative feedback. This is your chance to shine and to really demonstrate your independent writing skills. Chapter 13 outlines the requirements for writing an effective discussion chapter, and also focuses on preparing the final manuscript for submission of your dissertation.

12

Writing Style

By this point in your course, you will be familiar with many of the demands of academic writing. This chapter aims to consolidate your existing writing skills and provides guidance on skills that are key to producing your dissertation: namely, writing concisely and clearly, and generating 'flow'. It is also important to recognise the appropriate report-writing style for your dissertation, and to maintain this style consistently throughout your writing.

Learning outcomes

By the end of this chapter you will:

- Understand the dissertation as a scientific research report, and how it differs from your previous work
- Understand some of the expectations of academic writing
- Understand the importance of writing concisely and clearly
- Understand how to summarise and organise the discussion of literature to form a strong and effective argument
- Understand how to structure your work effectively to generate flow in your writing.

12.1 The dissertation as a scientific report, and how it differs from your previous work

Psychology, as an academic discipline, generally considers the scientific report as the most typical format for writing up a research project. Reporting the results of scientific empirical research projects, scientific reports usually consist of a literature review, methodology, analysis and results, and a detailed discussion of findings. Most psychology programmes expect students to have completed a number of psychological research reports as part of their assessed material over the first two stages of their degree pathway. As such, by the time you embark on your dissertation journey, you will have already become familiar with many of the requirements for producing a research report. You will understand the required elements of the report; be familiar with methods for searching the literature and reporting findings of a literature review; understand how to report research methodology; and have some level of understanding of data analysis and reporting of findings. Although this prior learning will stand you in good stead for applying this knowledge to your dissertation, it is also important to recognise that your tutors and examiners will therefore expect you to have mastered many of the principles of writing style, referencing and formatting, and to consolidate this prior learning to produce a high standard of work.

We must also consider that there are a number of crucial differences between the scientific reports that you will have produced previously and the dissertation:

1. Your dissertation will be considerably longer than any report you have written previously. As such, the writing style employed in your dissertation will likely differ from reports you have written in the past.

2. The style of study differs dramatically from previous assessments. Whilst you will have engaged in independent study in the past, the conduct of research reports at previous stages of your programme of study will likely have involved some element of group work, whether in the collection of data or the discussion of findings. For example, you may have collected data as a group, followed by writing up individual research reports (demonstrating the ability to work alongside other students when writing up similar projects), or you may have worked as a group to conduct a project, analyse your data and present your findings as a team of researchers. Both types of assessment are useful for developing your team working and research skills, but the dissertation is very different in nature, requiring independence throughout. Whilst your classmates will also be producing a scientific report for their dissertations, their projects will probably be very different from your own, so it is important that you are able to formulate your own style and tell your own story in your dissertation.

3. The design of your project may be very different from research designs you have been exposed to and used in your earlier assessments. As such, you may be exploring new elements of research methodology or using a new method of analysis that you are not familiar with, and it is important that you are able to report these elements effectively (see Chapters 6–8 for detail on methodology, and Chapters 10 and 11 on data analysis). Adhering to general standards such as those set out by the American Psychological

Association (APA) is a good place to start, as the vast majority of psychology courses will expect students to follow these guidelines in their academic work. We will cover APA guidelines in more detail later on in this chapter.

4. Finally, we should consider the flexibility of the topic of your dissertation. Your dissertation topic is one you have more control over in comparison to previous work. Whilst the topics of projects you will have completed at earlier stages of your course will likely have been chosen for you by your module tutors, the topic of your dissertation will be one which you have a vested interest in. Even if it's not a topic you have chosen yourself, it will be a project you have designed and conducted independently with the support of your project supervisor. At the write-up stage, it is therefore likely that you will have developed sufficient background knowledge to be able to discuss the topic area at length. Reporting the findings of the literature review concisely and coherently is therefore critical in creating an effective argument and producing a strong rationale for your project.

12.2 Academic writing

You've already completed many academic assessments, but what exactly is academic writing, and what do your examiners expect?

- Academic writing myth: Academic writing is a relatively simplistic proposition. It merely requires the consistent and unalterable overuse of unnecessarily loquacious verbiage in a transparent attempt to appear grandiosely intellectual and overwhelm the audience with incomprehensible psychological expertise.
- No! It is all about clarity! Academic writing is quite straightforward. It requires clear use of language in order to show the accuracy of the points being made and to ensure the reader is engaged with the work and its value in the field.

12.3 Writing clearly and concisely

Ensuring clarity and conciseness in your work can be difficult to achieve. You need to include a certain level of detail and explanation, but without waffling or going off topic. Your readers need to be able to understand your work – this includes your second marker and external examiners, who will not be as familiar with your project like your supervisor is – so your argument and message need to be clear.

```
                                                    ┌──────────────┐
                                                    │ EMPLOYABILITY │
                                                    │     TIP!      │
                                                    └──────╲  ╱─────┘
                                                            ╲╱
```

Being able to communicate your ideas clearly is a key skill that many employers will look for. Job criteria often include written and verbal communication skills, which your referees will likely be asked to comment on. Ensuring that you write clearly in your dissertation is an ideal opportunity to showcase your writing skills.

Your choice of appropriate terminology throughout your work will be important in ensuring that your writing is clear and understandable – random indiscriminate use of the thesaurus does not make for a good read! However, whilst you should try to ensure appropriate word and phrase choices for your readers, your work should maintain a scientific, professional and analytic tone. To achieve this, you should take note of appropriate grammar.

Grammar tips: Terminology, perspective and tense

- **Avoid colloquial language**: Don't write as you speak, and avoid unnecessary contractions of words.
- **Avoid use of technical jargon, at least without prior explanation**: This will confuse your readers – remember, you want to capture their attention and keep them interested.
- **Avoid writing in the first person**: Many academic disciplines generally consider the most appropriate perspective in your writing to be the third person – that is, 'The researcher chose to…', rather than the first-person perspective which would refer to 'I' or 'we'.
- **Write in the past tense, unless it is not appropriate**: When discussing a standardised assessment that is still available for use, for example, it would be more appropriate to write in the present tense – 'The Self-Esteem Scale consists of 24 items…'. Other than in these situations though, it would be appropriate to write the majority of your report in the past tense, as, by the time we read it, it will have already been done.

12.4 Creating a coherent argument and generating flow

Your first step in ensuring that your writing style is appropriate is to go back over your essays and reports from your modules so far. What feedback have you received? How could your writing improve? Use your feedback from previous work to inform your current writing. Throughout the dissertation module, your department will most likely offer you various opportunities for formative feedback on different sections of your dissertation report. Responding to formative feed-back is covered in more detail in Chapter 13, but it is important that you don't think of your formative assessment points as the only targets for producing drafts of your work. Instead, you should be constantly adapting your work, particularly your literature review, in order to accommodate new research into your topic area as you progress with your research. Making changes to drafts you think are good can often feel uncomfortable, but as your results evolve, you may well need to update your literature review to take account of new information. Whilst you can't change your hypothesis after the research has been conducted, your literature review and discussion chapters will need to have links between them in order to create a coherent argument throughout your dissertation.

As we discussed in Chapter 4, your literature review should break the discussion of literature into key points, with each point becoming a paragraph. Each paragraph should discuss one point and lead clearly into the next paragraph in order to generate flow within your writing. This structure is relevant for the later sections of your dissertation too. Overly long or underdeveloped paragraphs demonstrate a lack of clear thinking and a lack of in-depth analysis of points, so try to maintain a balance between conciseness and sufficient discussion of information.

In Chapter 4, we discussed the 'egg-timer' shape of the dissertation, focusing on how the literature review forms the upturned triangle at the top of the egg timer. One of the most effective ways to formulate a clear argument in your dissertation is to adhere to this egg-timer shape throughout your work, beginning broadly, narrowing focus and then discussing your methodology, findings and how your study has widened knowledge (Figure 12.1).

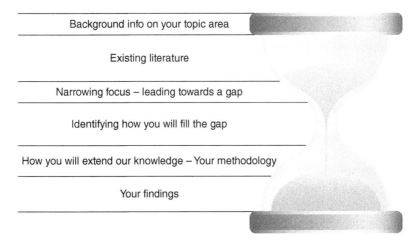

Background info on your topic area

Existing literature

Narrowing focus – leading towards a gap

Identifying how you will fill the gap

How you will extend our knowledge – Your methodology

Your findings

Figure 12.1 The 'egg timer' revisited

12.4.1 Paragraph structure and linking words

Throughout your dissertation, you need to ensure that your paragraphs follow a clear structure: each paragraph should link clearly to the preceding paragraph to form a logical discussion. Organising your discussion points logically and implementing effective transitions between paragraphs will help your reader to understand the argument you are trying to make. Paying careful attention to paragraph structure and links between paragraphs will demonstrate a thorough understanding of the literature, your project and how it relates to wider knowledge. Creating coherent links between paragraphs will also strengthen your argument and demonstrate good academic writing skills. Importantly, it will create flow in your writing – something which your examiners will be looking for. Figure 12.2 outlines some key linking words that you can use to strengthen your work; you should try to use a range of linking words and phrases between the points in your writing, rather than repeatedly using words like 'additionally' and 'furthermore'.

To add a point

- Also...
- In addition, ...
- Similarly, ...
- Not only..., but ... also
- Moreover, ...
- Furthermore, ...

To move on to the next point

- After this/that ...
- Subsequently, ...

To contrast two points

- However, ...
- Although ...
- On the other hand ...
- Conversely, ...
- In contrast, ...

To note consequences

- Therefore, ...
- As a result, ...
- Consequently, ...
- Despite ...

To illustrate, or to give an example

- For example, ...
- Clearly, ...
- That is, ...

To summarise or conclude

- Finally, ...
- In conclusion, ...
- To conclude, ...
- To summarise, ...

Figure 12.2   Terminology

12.4.2 Sentence structure and punctuation

Individual sentences should convey clear, individual points. Sentences which convey multiple clauses or are overly complex will be difficult to comprehend. It's therefore important to use punctuation appropriately to effectively communicate your points without losing your reader halfway through a sentence or between a series of shorter sentences. As supervisors, we often find ourselves commenting on students' inappropriate use of long sentences and suggest breaking these down into multiple shorter sentences to more effectively communicate a point. However, in some cases, longer sentences can be more effective (but not

too long to make your point unclear). Longer sentences tend to gradually introduce or more thoroughly explain a point, whereas shorter sentences tend to be
more abrupt. Using a series of short sentences one after another can be ineffective
and can make your writing seem disjointed. You can experiment with different
sentence lengths, depending on the type of point you are trying to make at the
time, but it is important to find a balance between different sentence lengths
throughout your work.

12.4.3 Linking your literature review to later sections of your report

Not only is it important to create logical links between your paragraphs and
sentences, but it is also important to ensure that there are logical links between
the different sections of your dissertation. The discussion of literature needs to
lead logically to the identification of a gap or rationale, which needs to lead

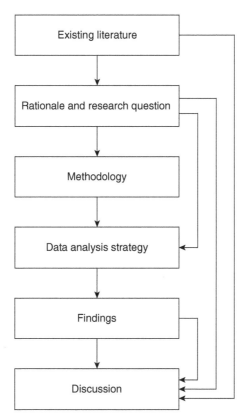

Figure 12.3   Flowchart demonstrating links between different sections of the
dissertation

logically to the identification of a suitable research question or aim for your project. Your research question needs to flow logically into the design of your project, which also needs to link logically to your chosen method of data analysis. Finally, the discussion chapter should tie all of this together to demonstrate your thorough and in-depth understanding of the story of your dissertation (Figure 12.3). Your ability to articulate this understanding in your writing will be critical for success in your dissertation.

12.5 Formatting and referencing: Adhering to APA (or other) guidelines

Most psychology courses will stipulate that students adhere in their academic work to the guidelines set out by the American Psychological Association (APA, 2019). The APA guidelines cover everything from referencing style to presentation of results and the formatting of tables and figures, so it is important to adhere to these standards throughout your work, including your results chapter. The APA guidelines also cover presentation of your written work including layout and the formatting of headings and subheadings.

Some departments and supervisors may be more strict than others regarding how closely they expect you to adhere to these guidelines, so it is important to discuss this with your supervisor at the earliest possible opportunity in order to adopt the most appropriate style from the earliest stage in your dissertation module. Some departments may prefer students to adhere to alternative styles of referencing – for example, Harvard style – so again check with your department or supervisor at the earliest opportunity. There are some similarities between the two, as many principles of APA referencing style are derived from the Harvard style, but it is also important to recognise the specificities of each style, and the expectations of your department in terms of how closely they expect you to adhere to these principles. It is also important to recognise from a publication perspective that psychological research may not always be published in psychological journals, and journals from other disciplines will often adopt very different styles – so don't be suprised if you come across a journal paper with a different formatting and/or referencing style to that which you are used to seeing (and using) in psychological research reports.

Chapter summary

In this chapter, we have discussed the skills that are key to producing your dissertation: namely, writing concisely and clearly, and generating 'flow'. We have briefly discussed APA formatting and the importance of ensuring clear links between the sections of your dissertation.

Checklist

✓ Proofread your work.

✓ Check that you have only one main point per paragraph.

✓ Check that you have included evidence to support your points.

✓ Check that all evidence is appropriately referenced.

✓ Proofread your work (again).

✓ Break any overly long sentences down.

✓ Check grammar and punctuation between sentences and points.

✓ Check paraphrasing and referencing.

✓ Check your linking words – do any need adding/changing/removing?

✓ Proofread your work (yes, again!)

✓ Check for typos.

✓ Eliminate jargon.

✓ Be concise.

✓ Proofread your work (once more for good measure!).

✓ Oh, and then proofread. Again.

13

Writing the Discussion Chapter and Preparing for Submission

The final chapter of the dissertation document is the discussion chapter. This is where you summarise and discuss your findings in relation to previous literature, your hypotheses and research aims, your theoretical perspective, future research and practical applications. The discussion gives you the opportunity to showcase your academic skills, and to demonstrate your understanding of the topic area, of your empirical findings and of the theory behind your project. In many institutions, the discussion is the only part of the dissertation on which you will not have an opportunity to receive formative feedback, and so it is the most independent piece of work in the whole dissertation. It is also probably the most important section of the dissertation as it summarises your findings, refines your focus and concludes the 'story' behind your project. This chapter will explore the seven key sections of a good discussion chapter. As the discussion chapter is the final section of your dissertation, we will also consider steps for preparing your final manuscript – how best to use and respond to formative feedback, and what needs to be included in the final dissertation submission. Bear in mind that your institution or department may have specific requirements for including alternative or additional sections in your final submission, so you should refer to your module guidance in conjunction with the information provided in this chapter.

Learning outcomes

By the end of this chapter you will:

- Understand the seven key components of a successful discussion chapter
- Understand how to use and respond to formative feedback
- Understand how to format your final dissertation and what to include for submission
- Understand some common formatting mistakes and how to avoid them in your final dissertation.

13.1 The seven key components of a good discussion chapter

1. Summarise your findings.
2. Relate your findings to your hypothesis/es and previous literature.
3. Attempt to explain your findings
4. Discuss the limitations of your methodology/project.
5. Discuss directions for future research.
6. Revisit the meaningful contribution of your project.
7. Consider the practical applications of your findings.

Let's consider each of these in turn.

13.1.1 Summarising your findings

The first section of the discussion chapter should be a summary of your findings. You shouldn't use statistics here; try instead to explain what you have found using words. Remember that by this point your reader will have read your introduction, so they will know what your research questions are. They will also have read your methodology, so they know how you have addressed your research questions. And, they will have read your results, so they know roughly what you have found. Now you need to give your account of how the research questions have been answered. So, in this section what we really want to see is a summary of what the findings are.

13.1.2 Relating your findings to the literature and your hypothesis/es

Once you have summarised your findings, you should think about how they relate to the literature you have discussed in the literature review. Did your findings support previous literature in the area? Also consider your hypothesis(es) and whether the data support or refute what you predicted. If you are conducting qualitative research, you will not have a hypothesis, but you can still discuss the relationship with the literature. If you had multiple aims or research questions, it may be worth breaking this section down to discuss each question in turn. The main purpose of this section is to account for your findings in relation to the literature and consider whether your findings were expected or not. In doing so, you should consider both empirical research findings and theoretical accounts of the topic area. How do your findings relate to theory as well as research?

Don't worry if your findings didn't support your hypothesis or the literature – this does not mean that you won't be able to produce a good discussion chapter. If this happens, your next job is to explain why this might have happened, and what the reasons are for getting the results you did.

13.1.3 Explaining your findings

As well as summarising your main findings, you must also be able to explain why your findings occurred. It's important to consider your theoretical perspective here, explaining why you believe you obtained the results you did. Consider why and how two particular variables might be related, why two groups of individuals might perform differently on a particular task, or why discussing a particular topic might give rise to particular themes. Regardless of your design or research questions, the key word here is 'why?'

13.1.4 Limitations of your methodology

Even though your theoretical perspective might provide a perfectly good explanation for why certain findings might have occurred, there will always be limitations which could have had an influence on the findings, and there will always be some parts of the research project that could benefit from improvement if the study was to be replicated. You should refer to these as limitations, not weaknesses: weaknesses in a design suggest that you didn't fully think through the design before conducting it, whereas limitations imply things that were relatively uncontrollable, such as access to participants and specific materials.

When you discuss the limitations of your study, you should make sure that you fully explain each of your points, elaborating on how each of these limitations could have influenced your findings. For example, if your sample was from a student population within a particular institution, you may conclude that the sample was not representative of a wider population. However, you need also to make sure you discuss the reasons why a different sample might have produced different results, thus explaining your theoretical perspective on the sample used. You might also conclude that the sample size was small, probably due to the time constraints of the dissertation. However, you should be wary of making statements such as this, as the module will have been designed to allow you time to conduct a scientific project; claiming that you ran out of time could therefore imply that you did not manage your time effectively. Instead, you could conclude that the population you were working with were difficult to access or recruit, but, as with the suggestions above, make sure that you are able to explain this and form a convincing argument. You also need to ensure that any limitations discussed are supported by relevant references to literature and/or theory. For example, if you are conducting a study looking at male and female attitudes towards relationships, you might conclude that the differences observed between groups could be due to confounding variables, such as culture. If, when discussing the limitations of your design, you make reference to there being differences between cultures, you need to ensure that you quote relevant literature to support this claim: claims are only relevant when supported by literature or theory.

EMPLOYABILITY TIP!

Discussing effectively the limitations of your study demonstrates your ability to critically evaluate your own work. Being able to think critically not only about existing research, but also about your own work, is an important transferable skill. Being able to suggest potential future directions also demonstrates your ability to identify solutions to remaining problems or gaps in knowledge.

13.1.5 Directions for future research

Once you have discussed and explained your findings and the limitations of your research, you should now consider how future research could build upon your work. Think of research as a *journey*. You started with what was already out there, found a gap in knowledge and tried to address this gap by conducting your project. Now that you have completed your project, further doors will open to new research ideas. Remember, scientific discoveries are incremental in producing new knowledge, so you need to try to be creative here, rather than just addressing the limitations you have discussed. Particularly if your findings have contradicted existing research or theory, there will be new questions that arise regarding the validity of theories, the replicability of your findings (perhaps under different conditions or in different populations), and so on.

13.1.6 Revisiting the meaningful contribution of your project

The meaningful contribution of your project should have been highlighted in the rationale at the end of the literature review. At this point in the discussion, you should reconsider this contribution, and discuss where your project has succeeded. Despite the limitations of your project, what contribution can your study make to the research literature and knowledge in the area? Taking your findings into consideration, what do we know now that we didn't know before? This is your chance to really sell your project to your readers and clarify the contribution that you have made to knowledge by conducting this piece of research.

13.1.7 Practical applications

Finally, you should consider how your findings could have an impact in the real world, and how the results of your study can be applied in research, knowledge or practice. For example, there may be implications for the medical profession, counselling or the NHS if you have conducted a clinical-type study or a qualitative interview. There may be implications for practice in schools, or to knowledge of child development and education if you have conducted a school-based project. There may be applications to applied areas of psychology, such as health, neurology, cognition, development, social, education or sport. You should try to consider how your findings can have an impact on our understanding of the topic area too, as this helps to emphasise the contribution of your project and adds to the selling point of your research.

Top tip!

Revisiting the meaningful contribution of your project in the discussion chapter helps to demonstrate and conclude the impact of your work. This concludes the 'story' of the dissertation, strengthening your message.

Homework

Start to make some notes for each section of the discussion chapter, structuring it into seven main sections. Remember, it is unlikely that you will be allowed to discuss your work on this section with your supervisor, so it is important that you invest a significant amount of time in writing and proofreading this chapter, ensuring that your argument is both strong and clearly communicated.

13.2 Preparing the final manuscript

As discussed above, the discussion chapter is the final chapter of your dissertation. Once you have written this, your next job will be to begin to prepare the final manuscript for submission. There are several things that you need to do during this process. Firstly, you will need to review and respond to the formative feedback that you have received from your supervisor on various sections of your work to date. Secondly, you will need to spend a significant amount of time proofreading, redrafting and formatting your work in line with APA guidelines. You will need to read and check your referencing, including both your in-text citations and your reference list. Do not wait for the submission deadline day to work on references, appendices and formatting – they always take longer than expected, and you need to leave time to proofread one last time before submission.

Top tip!

Work on referencing and formatting as you progress through the module – this will save you time at the end – and make sure you leave time to proofread your work before submission.

13.2.1 Editing your final dissertation: Responding to formative feedback

In order to achieve the best possible mark in your dissertation, it is advisable to follow the advice of your supervisor when it comes to editing your final manuscript. It is likely that your department will offer you opportunities to submit draft chapters of your dissertation for formative feedback from your supervisor at various points throughout the module, and it is important that you take this feedback on board and respond to it as best you can. However, as highlighted earlier, it is important that you don't think of your formative assessment points as the only opportunities for producing a draft of your work. Instead, you should be constantly adapting your work, particularly your literature review, in order to accommodate new research as you progress with your research. Making changes to aspects you think are good can often feel uncomfortable, but as your results evolve, you may well need to update your literature review to take account of new information. Of course, there may also be bigger changes that you need to make to the content and structure of your work, and your formative feedback will be instrumental in highlighting areas of good practice and areas for improvement.

The process of receiving and responding to formative feedback is very similar to the process you would go through in editing a manuscript for publication (see more in Chapter 14). When we submit a journal article for publication, the first step is for it to be reviewed by independent reviewers, and we then receive comments back on what can (and *should*) be amended. In a similar vein, formative feedback from your supervisor provides you with comments and advice on what can (and *should*) be amended in the final dissertation.

EMPLOYABILITY TIP!

Learning how to respond effectively to formative feedback during your dissertation module is really good practice for the publication process. The ability to respond to feedback is also a good employability skill.

The dissertation is probably the largest and most significant piece of work that you will complete during your university life, so it's fair to assume that you will want to make it the best it can possibly be. In order to achieve this, you will want to make sure that you have responded to every comment your supervisor has made and that you are completely happy with the standard of your submission. One way of doing this is to make a list of the comments you have received on each section of the dissertation – and include tips and advice from your module material too, if necessary. You can do this in a table, similar to Table 13.1.

Table 13.1   Responding to formative feedback

Feedback received (What do you need to work on?)	Action plan (What are you going to change?)	Support needed (What help will you need?)
Arguments made in my literature review were not always coherent	Use linking sentences effectively at start/end of all paragraphs	Online essay writing resources
I missed some spelling and grammatical errors	Allow time for proofreading (It can be helpful to insert a delay between writing and checking)	Could ask a friend to proofread my work and do the same for them

During the publication process, you'd be expected to respond to each comment from the reviewers and to illustrate how you have responded to these comments in an accompanying letter. Presenting this information in a table, like the one above, can be an effective way of ensuring that you respond to each comment sufficiently. It's unlikely that you'd be required to submit this table as a letter to your supervisor, explaining how you have responded to their comments, but it is good practice for the development of your dissertation. By responding to feedback in this way, you will ensure that you have responded to all of your formative feedback comments, giving you the best possible chance of success.

Homework

Complete the formative feedback table with your formative feedback comments and responses as you work through the feedback for the sections of your dissertation to date.

13.2.2 Formatting your dissertation

Once you are happy that you have responded sufficiently to all of your feedback comments, your next step will be to proofread your work and check your formatting throughout. Below, we have outlined some key issues and common mistakes with formatting that you should try to avoid.

The most common mistakes we observe students making with formatting their final dissertation are APA errors, including the following:

- Indents not used (you should include indents at the start of each paragraph in the main body, and a hanging indent in the reference list)
- Errors in formatting headings and subheadings
- Errors in tables and figures
- Inconsistencies and errors presenting in-text citations
- Citations not presented in alphabetical order (when multiple references are listed in parenthesis), and references not in alphabetical order in the reference list
- Missing information in the reference list
- Poor grammar and punctuation
- Spelling and typing errors
- Poor sentence structure
- Apostrophes used for quotations – use "quotation marks"
- Apostrophes, bold text and/or underlining used to emphasise a point – use *italics*
- Repeated openers to sentences and paragraphs, and/or poor flow between paragraphs.

Your final dissertation should be presented in Times New Roman (or similar), font size 12. The spacing between lines should be 1.5 or double, and you should use a first-line indent for the first line of every paragraph. An example of formatting is provided in Figure 13.1.

Prejudice is " ... an unjustified negative attitude toward an individual based solely on that individual's membership in a group" (Worchel, Cooper, & Goelthal, 1988, p. 449). However, as Fiske (2000) states "... thoughts and feelings do not exclude, oppress, and kill people; behaviour does" (p. 312). Thus, discrimination, defined as a means of "... limit[ing] or restrict[ing] access to privileges or resources by a minority group" (Stratton & Hayes, 1999, p. 79) warrants closer investigation if social psychologists wish to make a useful contribution to reducing prejudice.

Research establishing a relation between prejudice and discrimination is somewhat mixed. Some early research indicates a dissociation between the attitude of prejudice and

---

Figure 13.1   Example of formatting

Note: The formatting within this book does not necessarily follow APA guidelines.

13.2.3 Compiling your final manuscript

The next step in preparing your final manuscript is to bring together the individual chapters of the literature review, methodology, results and discussion, together with an abstract, references and relevant appendices. Below we have outlined the basic requirements for your final dissertation, but you should refer to the specific guidelines and requirements for your dissertation module to ensure that you have included everything necessary for your assessment.

What to include in the final dissertation

- Assessment cover sheet (if your institution uses one)
- Title page (use APA format)
- Author's declaration page (if required)
- Acknowledgments (optional)
- Abstract (150–250 words)
- Contents page
- Lists of tables and figures (if necessary)
- Literature review
- Methodology
- Results
- Discussion (sometimes, the results and discussion chapters can be combined in qualitative research, but speak to your supervisor about what would be the most appropriate presentation method for your dissertation)

(Continued)

- References
- Appendices (usually including a copy of participant-facing ethical forms such as the participant information sheet, consent form and debrief; evidence of ethical approval; and copies of any materials or measures used. Your institution may require additional documents to be appended).

Chapter summary

In this chapter, we have discussed how to write an effective discussion chapter for your dissertation, covering guidance on the seven key points that should be included.

We have discussed how to format and edit your final dissertation in line with formative feedback comments, and some of the common formatting mistakes that students make with their dissertations. Finally, we have provided guidance on what to include in the final manuscript.

Checklist

✓ Complete your discussion chapter, ensuring that you address each of the seven key points.

✓ Work through formative feedback, addressing comments as thoroughly as possible.

✓ Proofread your work.

✓ Check your work to ensure you have not made any mistakes with formatting.

✓ Proofread your work (again).

✓ Cross-check the contents of your dissertation against requirements for your module.

✓ Cross-check your in-text citations with your reference list.

✓ Proofread your work (one more time).

✓ Submit your work.

BEYOND THE DISSERTATION

The final part of this book focuses on the development of your dissertation into a journal article, conference poster or oral presentation.

14

Communicating Research: Preparing Manuscripts, Posters and Talks

Your dissertation is the first independent research project that you will have conducted, and it is something to be proud of! The dissertation builds upon the teaching and assessments you have completed as part of your research methods modules throughout the course, and really consolidates your knowledge and experience of research design and methodology into a piece of work that you have worked on independently throughout the course of your final year of studies. Once you have completed and submitted your dissertation and have received a mark for your work, you may be thinking about the possibility of publishing your research. If this is something you are aiming for, then read on! The final chapter of this book is centred on disseminating your findings in the real world and preparing your dissertation for publication. This chapter also covers guidance for preparing for presentation at conferences, including some tips on preparing an effective poster and/or conference talk.

Learning outcomes

By the end of this chapter you will:

- Understand the value of disseminating your research findings
- Have an understanding of the key differences and similarities between your dissertation document and a journal paper

- Understand the process of publication
- Understand basic requirements for conference presentations, including posters and oral presentations.

14.1 Forms of dissemination

Researchers disseminate their research findings in all kinds of different ways. The most common ways of 'getting your research out there' are to publish a paper in an academic journal or to present at a conference. Many researchers work with organisations in the community and may also present their findings directly to the relevant parties, or may engage with the media via news articles, blogs, social media and marketing materials, sharing their expertise to explain social situations, problems and solutions. Ultimately, the way in which you decide to disseminate your research will depend on the type of message or story you want to tell, what audience you want to target and the availability of your options in terms of publication outlets. Academically, writing a manuscript for publication, presenting a poster and preparing a talk are the three key methods of communication amongst scientific researchers, and we will discuss each of these forms of dissemination in more detail later in this chapter.

Publishing myth

You can't get your dissertation published if you get a poor mark/don't get a first.

Incorrect. Whilst many supervisors would be wary of suggesting publication of poor quality work, getting a 2:2 (or even a 3rd) doesn't necessarily mean that your research shouldn't be published, it just means that it will require substantially more work to bring it to publishable standards compared to a dissertation that achieved a first-class mark. However, you should note that some work *is* unlikely to be published, if, for example, the design is weak or unjustified, questions are not rooted in psychological literature, or there is a poor rationale for your project. For this reason, it is important to think about the importance of careful planning throughout your dissertation module. It is also important to recognise that just because someone achieved a first-class mark, it doesn't mean that their work is necessarily worthy of publication. Publishing depends on a multitude of different factors, including writing style, the relevance of your work to the journal you choose to submit to and the story your work tells – is there a clear message to your project? Importantly, you should think about the *added value* of your project to knowledge in the field.

14.2 Planning for publication

Having your research published in an academic journal is the epitome of academic success, and having your name on a publication is a pretty amazing thing to put on your CV! If this is something you want to aim for, it is important to start planning early; publication is a lengthy process and doesn't happen overnight. If you're still studying your dissertation module at the time you're reading this, there are a few things you can be doing to prepare yourself for the process of publication later on:

- **Work hard, aim high**: As highlighted above, getting a high grade for your dissertation does not necessarily mean that your work is of publishable standard. There will be considerable work to do to format your work for publication in a journal, regardless of how closely you have adhered to APA formatting guidelines in your dissertation. But working hard and aiming to write the best possible dissertation you can are a good starting point.
- **Grasp APA formatting**: The vast majority of psychological journals will require you to format your work in line with APA guidelines. This doesn't just include referencing, but also things like presentation, headings, subheadings, tables and writing style. Grasping the basics of APA style from an early stage will mean that you have to do less work later on. If your university uses APA style, then you should already be familiar with the basic principles, but either way, our advice is to get a copy of the latest APA publication manual (2019) and adhere to it as closely as possible.
- **Strengthen your rationale**: One of the key components of a successful dissertation, and a successful paper, is having a strong, clear rationale for the project. Your rationale is the reason for doing what you are doing, so understanding this, and being able to explain it clearly, are key to the message you are trying to communicate. As you progress with your dissertation, continually ask yourself 'Why?' in response to every decision you make. Making sure that you can justify all of these decisions is important in strengthening your rationale, and this is something that you will have to communicate clearly in any resulting publication.
- **Understand your findings**: We cannot stress this enough! Being able to communicate effectively the findings of your research is just as important as the findings themselves, if not more important. This is because your ability to explain them effectively – in relation to previous literature, theory, your hypothesis (if relevant) and what they mean – demonstrates your level of understanding. This is important in the marking of your dissertation, but also for prospective reviewers and audience members. If you explain something clearly, it shows that you understand it.
- **Keep hold of your raw data**: Your institution will normally require you to keep hold of your raw data (stored in accordance with current data protection regulations) until the final mark for your dissertation has been released. If you're hoping for publication, however, many journals will require you to keep your raw

data file and some will ask you to supply this file as part of your submission, so make sure that you keep it safe. You'll need to make sure that you have thought about publication ethics in your ethical approval application too and that participants have been informed that their data may be published (subject to anonymisation, of course).

- **Talk to your supervisor and build a professional working relationship – they will be your collaborator**: This is perhaps the most important piece of advice that we can give you. Up until this point, your supervisor has acted in a purely supervisory capacity, providing advice and guidance on the design and conductance of your dissertation project. Ultimately, they will be marking your dissertation, so until your final marks have been released, they have a professional role to uphold as your supervisor. Once your marks have been released, if you decide to aim for publication, your supervisor will become your collaborator. As you will learn later on in this chapter, the process of publication can be lengthy and laborious, so it is not something that is going to happen overnight, or even within a few months. You'll need to keep in touch with your supervisor and to form a professional working relationship beyond that which was required for the dissertation module. Talk to them before you graduate and explain your intention to publish your work. As an academic and researcher, they will have experience of the publication process and will be able to offer you honest and realistic advice. They'll also have experience of writing for publication, so they may offer to help edit or rewrite sections of your work. When you are ready to submit your paper to a chosen journal, it is generally expected that you would include your supervisor as an author, so their name will be on the paper as well as yours. The order in which authors appear on the paper should reflect their level of contribution to the project and the final written report. Generally, if you have designed and run your own project, and rewritten the paper for publication largely independently, then your name should appear as the lead author. However, if you have completed a project suggested by your supervisor for your dissertation, and/or they have made a large contribution to the writing of the final paper, then you should be prepared to list them as the lead author. Either way, it would be courteous to have a conversation with your supervisor early on to discuss the level of contribution that you both plan to make to the final submission and the order that author names will appear on the paper.

EMPLOYABILITY TIP!

Having your research published in an academic journal is the epitome of academic success and having your name on a publication is a pretty amazing thing to put on your CV! Make sure you mention this in job applications and interviews – publication shows that you have not only succeeded in your academic work but have also had an influence on knowledge in the wider field.

14.3 The publication process

Step 1: Choose an appropriate journal to submit to

The first step in publication is deciding which journal you want to submit to. One of the most common reasons for rejection is that researchers submit their paper to an inappropriate journal for their work. It is important to make sure you do plenty of research into appropriate journals in your field of study, and read some papers from each of them to determine whether the design, methodology, analysis and findings of your own research are reflective of the scope of the journal. A good starting point would be to look at the key papers you have read and reported on in your literature review – where have they been published? A lot of journal webpages are freely accessible without having to create an account, so you should be able to access author guidelines and publication information without having to commit to making a submission. Look at the most recent issues of those journals to see what types of project papers have been published, to find a journal that fits best with your paper.

Another consideration when choosing a journal is its **impact factor**. This is used to place journals in a hierarchy, with the higher-ranking journals having a higher impact factor rating. The impact factor of a journal is based on the number of citations that a journal has received in any one year (i.e. the number of times that other publications have cited articles published in that journal). Whilst it is useful to be aware of impact factors when looking at potential journals for your paper, it is also important to be aware that (a) the impact factor of a journal can change from year to year, as citation numbers change (so make sure you check the most up-to-date figures), and (b) some of the most impactful research is published in highly specialised journals (and often, *special issues*), which may have a seemingly low impact factor in comparison to bigger, more well-known journals.

Step 2: Meet author guidelines and edit your paper

Sadly, you won't be able to publish your dissertation in its original format – but it *is* a good starting point. Once you have selected a journal that seems to be appropriate for your research article, the first thing to do will be to download and read the author guidelines. Journals have slightly different requirements for the documents that need to be submitted and the format that they need to be submitted in. For example, most journals will ask you to submit a separate cover sheet with the article title and author information, such that the main article is anonymous for the reviewers. The journal will have a specific format in which this information needs to be presented, and this should be outlined in the author guidelines. Some journals will ask for additional documents with highlights of the paper, and some will ask for a separate document containing the abstract.

Importantly, make sure you look at the word limit for the journal – many journals will have a limit of between 3,000 and 5,000 words. This is likely to be much shorter than your original dissertation document, so you will need to do some substantial editing to meet this limit.

Step 3: Craft and proofread your article

Craft your work so that your line of argument and your meaningful contribution are clear, and your methodology and findings are transparent. Proofreading is key to being confident in your submission. Make sure you give yourself plenty of time to proofread for typos and grammatical errors, as well as for consistency in your terminology and writing style throughout. Try and get at least one other person to proofread it too – someone independent of you and your supervisor. If someone who is not familiar with the project can understand your article, this will save you answering clarification questions from reviewers at a later date.

Step 4: Submit your article

Once you are happy with your final article and have prepared all supplementary documentation, you are ready to submit. You will need to create an author account with the relevant journal to set up your submission. Once you have submitted, your article will go through the process of review by independent reviewers. Reviewers will usually be two or three experts in the subject area of your paper (or as close as possible). They will provide a thorough review of the full paper, providing both general and specific comments throughout. Each reviewer will make a recommendation as to whether they believe the paper should be published in this journal, and whether they think it needs any amendments or additions. These recommendations will be sent back to the editor, who will then make a decision. It is important to be aware that this review process can often be quite lengthy – reviewers are usually active researchers themselves, and are often academics with busy day-to-day lives, who will need to fit in the review of your paper around their own work. The length of time that they are given to review your paper will vary depending on the journal, but it's important to be aware that you could be waiting anything up to six months for a decision.

Step 5: Receive a decision

Following the review process, you will receive comments from the reviewers and a decision from the editor on whether or not the journal will publish the article. Your decision will usually be one of the following:

Your article is accepted

It is unlikely that your paper will be accepted without any amendments at all, as this usually indicates low standards of reviewing, particularly for larger journals.

Your article is accepted pending minor or major amendments (revise and re-submit)

If you receive a 'revise and re-submit' decision, your next job will be to work through the comments from your reviewers and respond to each comment in turn, making changes to the manuscript where necessary. These may be minor changes in places, such as changing the wording or editing the formatting. However, some changes are likely to be more substantial, and it is not unusual to be asked to re-analyse data (another reason to keep hold of your raw data file!) or to rewrite entire sections of the report. Sometimes, you might receive a decision that your article has been rejected, but the editor may welcome a re-submission. This can be confusing, but essentially what it means is that the article is unpublishable in its current form and major revisions are required for it to be reconsidered for publication. Depending on the level of amendments required, you will be given different lengths of time in which to complete the revisions and re-submit your article. Typically, minor amendments will need to be completed in 3–6 months, whilst major amendments will need to be completed in 6–12 months, but the length of these periods will vary depending on the journal.

Your article is rejected

It is bound to be disappointing if your article is rejected. There are various reasons why you might receive this outcome – for example, the journal may be oversubscribed with submissions, or the reviews may be negative (sometimes over-critical) despite the editor seemingly being keen on your paper. It is often difficult to judge what these outcomes mean for your paper, particularly if you receive a rejection. It's important to recognise that different journals have different standards to uphold and will receive varying numbers of submissions at any one time. Journals have a limit on how many papers they can publish at once, and different journals will have different numbers of issues every year, each of which will be limited in the number of papers it can publish. Some of the more popular journals will therefore have to reject large numbers of papers simply because they don't have space to publish them all, but because of this they can afford to be selective, and standards are likely to be higher. The important thing to remember is that this is all part of the process – if you get knocked back, don't give up, and try again somewhere else. Importantly though, you can only submit to one journal at a time. When you submit, you will be asked to confirm that the article has not been submitted or published elsewhere, so, until you get a rejection or withdraw your paper from one journal, you cannot submit it anywhere else.

Step 6: Respond to reviewer comments

As discussed above, it's unlikely that your paper will get accepted outright without any amendments being required. If your paper is accepted pending minor or major amendments, or if your paper is rejected but the editor would welcome a re-submission, you will need to think about how you will edit your article in preparation for re-submission. The feedback that you have received from the reviewers is valuable at this stage in helping you to understand what improvements can (and *should*) be made to the original article. When you re-submit your paper, you will also be expected to submit a letter explaining how you have responded to the reviewers' comments, so you will need to think about how you will demonstrate that you have considered their comments and implemented their advice. So how do you prepare for this process? Well, as we discussed in Chapter 13, this is similar to the process of receiving and responding to formative feedback from your supervisor during the dissertation module. Importantly, by following the process we outlined in Chapter 13 on responding to formative feedback, you will also be preparing yourself for the process of responding to reviewer comments during the publication process. Figure 14.1 provides an example of a similar table to that presented in section 13.2.1, which might be created as part of the process of responding to reviewer comments:

Dear Editor and Reviewers,

Thank you for accepting our paper entitled "The Immediate and Longer Term Effectiveness of a Speech Rhythm-Based Reading Intervention for Beginning Readers" for publication in the Journal of Research in Reading. Please see our responses to the comments from the Associate Editor and Reviewers below. We hope that this meets with your expectations and look forward to hearing from you soon regarding publication.

Comments from	Comments	Authors' Response
Associate Editor	I wondered what happened to the internal reliabilities for the tests – I could not find them in this version of the paper.	The internal reliabilities for the tests have now been added using Cronbach's alpha.
	A few typos	The manuscript has been proofread and checked for typos.

Figure 14.1   Responding to reviewer comments

14.4 Your dissertation and how it is similar to a journal article

It's not just the process of responding to feedback in your dissertation module that is similar to the publication process. Your dissertation is similar to a journal article in a number of ways. For example, your dissertation contains all the key sections of a journal paper, such as a literature review, methodology, results and discussion. The main difference is that your dissertation will probably be much longer than the limit for a journal article, so, although your dissertation will contain the correct subsections, it will require substantial editing in order to be much more concise and to meet the word limit of the journal you plan to submit to. It is also worth noting that the vast majority of journals will require you to adhere to the APA (2019) formatting and referencing style. Many institutions already use APA formatting, which means that you will be required to adhere to the standards stipulated by the APA for presentation and writing style within your assessed work. If your institution does not use APA, it is likely that they will use a similar system such as Harvard, so you should be familiar with some of the basic principles of writing academically. You can find out more about academic writing style in Chapter 11 and we would encourage you to review this if you are thinking about publication.

14.5 Conferences

Attendance and presentation at an academic conference is perhaps the most effective way of instantly communicating your research and findings to other academics, students, researchers and experts in the field. Conferences are also a good option if you do not feel ready to submit your work for publication in a journal, as they give you an opportunity to discuss your work with other researchers in the field and potentially get some valuable feedback from them in advance of aiming to publish a formal paper. Many researchers present their work at conferences before their papers are published, so conferences are a great way to gain up-to-date knowledge about recent and ongoing research in the field. Conferences also give you a great opportunity to network with others who are researching a similar area to yours, and possibly to meet some of the researchers whose work you have read and cited in your dissertation!

14.5.1 Choosing a conference and applying to present

There are thousands of conferences for all the different areas of psychology, so choosing an appropriate conference at which to present your work can sometimes be difficult. Conferences take many formats and they vary greatly in size, length, budget, costs and standards. They may be small local group meetings, large national conferences, or international conferences with thousands of delegates. It is important to consider what is suitable for you, your budget, your ability to travel and your time. As you become accustomed to conference culture, you may find that there is a particular conference that you enjoy and gain the most from, but to start off with it can be difficult to identify the most suitable conference for you, and to know what to expect. A great place to start is the British Psychological Society, which holds annual conferences for individual divisions, some classified by the area of psychology they specialise in and some by region of the UK. The BPS also has specialised conferences for students, which would be a great starting point for presenting your dissertation.

Generally, there are two main ways of presenting your research at conferences: by presenting a poster or by giving a talk. When you apply to present at a conference, you will usually have to submit the title and an abstract for your presentation. You will have prepared an abstract for your dissertation submission, so you won't have to write one from scratch, but you may want to edit it to map on accurately to the requirements of the conference. Of course, once you have submitted your application to present at the conference, there is no guarantee that your presentation will be accepted. Applying to present at a large international conference can often be quite a competitive process, as there will only be so much space within the programme, particularly if you are intending to present a talk.

14.5.2 Posters

Poster sessions tend to take place in a communal space where there will be numerous poster boards with posters displayed from a range of researchers. Poster sessions usually have a timetabled slot on conference schedules, where delegates gather to look at the posters and speak to the author(s) to find out more. At most conferences, the poster sessions are quite informal, so it *appears* to put less pressure on presenters. We say 'appears' because presenting a poster might seem like an easy option – and it certainly might seem less daunting to start with – but it's important to be aware that presenting a poster can often require much more preparation. Poster sessions give delegates more time to browse and criticise the research of the author, and more time to ask questions than in an oral presentation where you would be limited in time to respond to questions and comments. You'll also need to stand by your poster for a long period of time – whereas the typical conference talk would be no longer than 20 minutes, poster sessions are likely to last one to two hours at a time. This means that you're likely to get lots of delegates who come and speak to you about the same topic and ask the same questions, so you find that you repeat yourself. It's also difficult to anticipate the questions you will be asked, so you need to be prepared to answer questions on the spot and be confident in having a spontaneous, and often critical, discussion about your research, repeatedly with various people within a short space of time.

So how do you create a conference poster? The format of conference posters can vary depending on the requirements of the specific conference, but most conference organisers stipulate that the poster needs to be either A1 or A0 in size. They often have a preference either for landscape or for portrait posters. A good poster will summarise all of the main sections of your project by providing an overview of existing literature that has led to the project, a clear rationale, research question(s) and hypothesis (if relevant), an overview of the methodology, a description of the key findings and a few key discussion points.

Poster presentations: What to include

1. Title
2. Introduction to the topic area (be concise!)
3. Your rationale and research question(s)
4. Your methodology – design, participants, materials, procedure
5. Your findings
6. Conclusions and practical applications – what does this mean in the real world?
7. Key references.

Top tips for creating and presenting a poster

Make your poster eye-catching and easy to read: The important thing to bear in mind is that it is not a written piece of work. It is intended to be eye-catching and easy to read, so make sure that your font size is suitable for people to be able to read from a couple of feet away. Your reader should be able to grasp the message in a couple of minutes – so don't include too much text. Bullet points are acceptable for many sections and should be easier to read than lengthy prose.

Make sure you are prepared: Although it is impossible to completely predict what questions you are likely to be asked, you can make a good guess by looking back over the feedback from your dissertation. Was anything unclear? Did your marker(s) identify any unanswered questions? Speak to your supervisor (see below) – they will be able to help you prepare for your presentation. Your university might also offer an opportunity for you to have a practice

(Continued)

run – if there is a research conference or dissertation conference that you can attend at your university, take the opportunity to practise. On the day, come with handouts – conference delegates will probably have a lot of posters that they want to see in one poster session, so give them something to take away to remember your work by.

Seek your supervisor's advice: Your supervisor will have had experience of conference presentations and so they will be able to provide you with some valuable advice about what to include in your poster, what to expect during the session, what questions you are likely to be asked and how to approach difficult questions.

14.5.3 Conference talks

If you choose to give an oral presentation, you will often be delivering it in a lecture theatre, conference suite or classroom-type space. The size of the space will depend on the size of the conference, the number of delegates and the programme structure – for example, if there are lots of parallel sessions, it is likely that each session will be in a smaller space, but this is largely dependent on the individual conference. The size of your audience will also vary greatly depending on these same variables of size and programme structure. The characteristics of your space and audience will also vary depending on how the talks are scheduled – at many conferences, oral presentations will be grouped into what we call 'symposia'. Each one will have its own topic, and there will usually be four or five short talks within each symposium. This is a good way of grouping talks on similar topics. Other conferences (usually smaller ones) will schedule talks in individual timeslots throughout the conference programme. Generally, you can expect that you will stand at the front and present your work to the audience, often using PowerPoint slides to illustrate your work whilst you talk.

Individual conferences have different requirements for oral presentations. Some may provide guidelines on the presentation of information on your slides, or on the structure of the talk, whilst others may be more relaxed and flexible. In general, you can expect that most oral presentations will be a maximum of 20 minutes in length, and this will often include time for questions, so you will only be speaking for around 15 minutes. You will be surprised how quickly this time disappears once you start talking, so try not to include too much information or too many slides. You want your audience to be captivated by your talk, so make it interesting, and make sure the key message is clear. Remember the importance of the rationale? Well, here is your chance to show it off! Your job as a speaker is to convince your audience that your project is worth listening to.

Oral presentations: What to include

1. A brief overview of the topic area
2. Your rationale – what gap are you addressing and why?
3. Your methodology – what did you do?
4. Your findings
5. A few key discussion points
6. Time for questions.

Top tips for oral presentations

- **Be clear and concise**: Earlier on in this chapter, we explained how important it is to make sure that you fully understand your rationale and your findings, and how important it is to be able to explain these aspects of your study clearly. Making sure you do this in your talk will capture your audience's attention and ensure that you get your message across.
- **Don't overcrowd your slides**: Similarly to a poster presentation (see section 14.5.2), your audience need to be able to read the information on your slides quickly. They are there to listen to you talk about your project, not to read extensive information from the screen. Similarly, don't include too many slides, as you may be tempted to go off at a tangent and go over your time allocation.
- **Be prepared**: Make sure you practise your presentation – in front of the mirror, in front of your family, in front of your supervisor. Take every opportunity to practise your talk and make sure that you are confident in what you are saying, and that you are comfortable with your timing. As mentioned in the poster section above, your university may offer opportunities for you to present your work at their own dissertation conference or research conference – this would be a great opportunity for you to practise your presentation in a familiar environment.

Chapter summary

In this chapter, we have discussed the value of disseminating your research findings, and how your dissertation lends itself to different types of dissemination. We have discussed the process of publication, and how to develop your dissertation into a journal article. Finally, we have discussed the basic requirements for conference presentations, including posters and oral presentations. You should use this information, alongside feedback and advice from your supervisor, to prepare for these processes of dissemination.

Checklist

✓ Check that you have ethical approval for the publication of your findings.

✓ Consider the different forms of dissemination and decide which to aim for: a journal publication, a poster presentation or an oral presentation.

✓ Check your understanding of your analysis and findings.

✓ Go over your feedback for your final dissertation and address any outstanding issues.

✓ Select an appropriate outlet for your work – that is, a specific journal or conference.

✓ Check relevant deadline dates for submissions.

✓ Check the requirements of the chosen outlet and edit your work accordingly.

✓ Submit your work for review.

References

American Psychological Association. (2019). *Publication Manual of the American Psychological Association*, Seventh Edition. Washington, DC: American Psychological Association.

Braun, V. & Clarke, V. (2006). Using thematic analysis in psychology. *Qualitative Research in Psychology*, 3(2), 77–101.

British Psychological Society. (2014). *Code of Human Research Ethics*. Leicester: BPS. www.bps.org.uk/sites/www.bps.org.uk/files/Policy/Policy%20-%20Files/BPS%20Code%20of%20Human%20Research%20Ethics.pdf

British Psychological Society. (2017). *Ethics Guidelines for Internet-Mediated Research*. Leicester: BPS. www.bps.org.uk/sites/www.bps.org.uk/files/Policy/Policy%20-%20Files/Ethics%20Guidelines%20for%20Internet-mediated%20Research%20%282017%29.pdf

British Psychological Society. (2018). *Code of Ethics and Conduct*. Leicester: BPS. www.bps.org.uk/news-and-policy/bps-code-ethics-and-conduct

Glaser, B. G. & Strauss, A. L. (1967). *The Discovery of Grounded Theory: Strategies for Qualitative Research*. Chicago: Aldine.

Harrison, E., Wood, C., Holliman, A., & Vousden, J. (2018). The immediate and longer-term effectiveness of a speech-rhythm-based reading intervention for beginning readers. *Journal of Research in Reading*, 41(1), 220–241.

Levene, H. (1960). Robust tests for equality of variances. In I. Olkin (ed.), *Contributions to Probability and Statistics*. Stanford, CA: Stanford University Press, 278–292.

Likert, R. (1932). A technique for the measurement of attitudes. *Archives of Psychology*, 22(140), 1–55.

McCallin, A. & Nayar, S. (2012). Postgraduate research supervision: A critical review of current practice. *Teaching in Higher Education*, 17, 63–74.

Rosenberg, M. (1965). *Society and the Adolescent Self-Image*. Princeton, NJ: Princeton University Press.

Strauss, A. & Corbin, J. M. (1990). *Basics of Qualitative Research: Grounded Theory Procedures and Techniques*. Newbury Park, CA: Sage Publications.

Stroop, J. R. (1935). Studies of interference in serial verbal reactions. *Journal of Experimental Psychology*, 18, 643–662.

Index

Note: Figures and tables are indicated by page numbers in bold print.

Printed in the USA
CPSIA information can be obtained
at www.ICGtesting.com
LVHW070627261223
767415LV00011B/490